The LIFE BEYOND

Ray Summers

The LIFE
BEYOND

BROADMAN PRESS
Nashville, Tennessee

© 1959 · BROADMAN PRESS
Nashville, Tennessee
All rights reserved
International copyright secured

4216–08

ISBN: 0–8054–1608–0

Library of Congress catalog card number 59–5863
Printed in the United States of America

To
My Wife
JESTER
alias
MARGARET!

Preface

N O APOLOGY is offered for presenting another book on eschatology. It is a fervent hope that it will prove to be not merely another book on eschatology but one which may make some contribution. Indeed, this volume was promised in 1951 in a work on Revelation, *Worthy Is the Lamb*. In that book the author proposed a subsequent volume in which he would deal specifically with other areas of eschatology—death, resurrection, the second coming, judgment, and eternal destiny. Many inquiries have come from many parts of the world about the completion of the promised work. Many requests, too, have come from friends and students that the work be finished. This is the fulfilment of that promise. It is released with a prayer that it may be of help to many who search for help and find only confusion when they study this important area of Christian truth.

This is a day when man's reasonably comfortable and permanent world has become uncomfortable, and the prospects for permanence at times seem remote. In such a day and under such conditions thinking men naturally turn their eyes to scan the horizon for signs of hope. In a day when all that can be shaken is being shaken, what may one know of that which cannot be shaken: God's ultimate purpose and provision for man?

"If," in the words of Paul, "the earthly house of our tabernacle be dissolved" (2 Cor. 5:1)—if, in the words of Peter, "the elements shall be dissolved with fervent heat and the earth and the works which are in it shall be burned up" (2 Peter 3:10)—if this *should* become reality, men of faith have ever held that it would not bring an end to existence. Man is not so earth bound that he cannot hope for God's promised "new heavens and a new earth, in which righteousness dwells permanently" (2 Peter 3:13). The aim of this book is to aid in man's quest for knowledge of the future as it is revealed in the New Testament.

The sources which have been most helpful will be indicated in the documentation. Grateful appreciation is accorded my friends and colleagues with whom many delightful and stimulating hours of discussion and debate have been spent. Grateful appreciation is accorded the Baptist Temple in Houston, Texas. Their liberality in the form of a recording machine has made this research much easier than it could otherwise have been. It should be noted here that throughout the book (except in one or two cases which are indicated) the translation of the Scriptures is my own.

RAY SUMMERS

Fort Worth, Texas

Contents

The *LIFE BEYOND*

Of the World to Come

We believe that the end of this world is approaching; that at the last day Christ will descend from heaven, and raise the dead from the grave to final retribution; that a solemn separation will then take place; that the wicked will be adjudged to endless punishment, and the righteous to endless joy; and that this judgment will fix forever the final state of men in heaven or hell, on principles of righteousness.

—From the Articles of Faith of Southwestern Baptist Theological Seminary, adapted from the New Hampshire Confession of Faith

Introduction

THE TERM "eschatology" is derived from two Greek words, ἔσχατος and λόγος. ἔσχατος is an adjective meaning "last"; it conveys the sense of the extreme, that which is last in place or in time. The word λόγος is a noun which has several usages. In the word "eschatology" it indicates a doctrine, a teaching, or a matter of discussion or dispute. Eschatology, then, is the doctrine of last things. This doctrine relates to a series of subjects which have to do with the consummation of human experience both in the world order and in the eternal order. The subjects usually treated in a study of eschatology are death, resurrection, the interim between death and resurrection, the second coming of Christ, judgment, eternal destiny, and the kingdom of God. There are other related subjects, but these are central.

A comparative survey of the religions of the world indicates that there is a place for eschatology in all of them. The varying tenets of the religions call for varying views of the subject, but the doctrine is present in each one. On the subjects of death, immortality, and eternal destiny there are many common ideas. On the other hand, some differences are more marked than the similarities. By its very nature a religion presupposes an eschatology.

What is the place of eschatology in the Christian religion?

1

The answer a person gives depends altogether upon his point of view and place in history. Those who hold that the New Testament is a book of authority must, however, make a place in their thinking for eschatology because it is unquestionably a part of the New Testament. One who rejects the authority of the New Testament may either accept or reject eschatology.

There was a time when eschatology was one of the main branches of theology. As such, it took its place with Christology, ecclesiology, soteriology, anthropology, pneumatology, and demonology. In many circles of Christian thought today it no longer holds such a position. In others eschatology is a most prominent subject of investigation and discussion. Chad Walsh [1] has made a discerning appraisal of the present situation with reference to eschatology. He observes that it requires patience today to find someone preaching on the resurrection of the body, final judgment, or a non-atomic end of the world. If one searches long enough and in the right places, Mr. Walsh says, he may find such a sermon.

Mr. Walsh suggests that there are four popular viewpoints regarding eschatology. He holds that orthodox theology "embalms" eschatology by accepting the Nicene Creed but conveniently pushing the events which this creed names into some remote future and leaving man comfortably situated in his reasonably permanent world. The orthodox statement on eschatology as it appears in the statement of the Councils of Nicaea, Constantinople, and Chalcedon is this: ". . . he shall come again, with glory, to judge the quick and the dead; whose kingdom shall have no end." "Gospel hall" theology busies itself with setting deadlines for the fulfilment of New Testament teachings on eschatology. These deadlines fail to bring the promised fulfilment, and the proponent must then shift his date to the safer future. Modernist theology explains away

[1] Chad Walsh, "Last Things, First Things," *Theology Today*, VI (April, 1949), 25–26.

2

the so-called hard sayings of Jesus and Paul and leaves no legitimate place for eschatology. Schweitzer's theology holds that Christ accepted the world view of his day and hence was mistaken in looking for a catastrophic end to the world.

This analysis of twentieth-century thinking on the subject of eschatology stimulates serious consideration and gives occasion for pointed questions. Is this a full picture of the situation? Do any of these viewpoints represent the thinking of those who wrote the New Testament? Does the New Testament conform either to a policy of looking to a remote and comfortable future or setting deadlines for the fulfilment of prophecy? Does not the New Testament affirm belief in the Lord's return and a consummation of God's purpose in the affairs of men but stop short of the deadline setting of "gospel hall" eschatology? Such questions can be answered only by close and honest study of the New Testament.

It must be admitted that where eschatology is concerned ours is a confused world. Many Christians are indifferent to the subject. On the other hand, a multitude of believers divides itself into two groups: one which claims to know the truth and another which is seeking that knowledge. There are people who are seeking, either from curiosity or devout interest, some certainty in the realm of death and that which follows or in the realm of man's destiny and God's purpose. Many are those who claim to have the answer. In too many instances, however, their answer is based upon some prejudiced viewpoint supported by a series of proof texts which may be forced to fit the position held. A casual survey of the religious page of the Saturday newspaper or a slow turn of the radio dial on Sunday morning will illustrate this truth.

What is to be done? The need is too great to be ignored. The only safe conduct through the maze of opinion and question is that afforded by the New Testament; here is the only adequate answer. To follow that course two things are necessary: first, one must understand what the New Testament teaches; second, one must accept that teaching and govern thought and conduct by it. The second of these is a matter which is entirely individual in scope. In the first, an understanding of the New Testament, one person may help another in the process of investigation and exchange of ideas. It is to that end that this book is devoted.

This work is a study of New Testament teachings on death, the disembodied state, the resurrection, the second coming of Christ, final judgment, and eternal destiny.[2] While the study of many books on the subject is in the background of the treatment, the work itself will be largely an exposition of the Scripture passages involved. There will be only limited quotations from authorities. It is to be hoped that by this procedure we may come to an understanding of what the New Testament teaches on eschatology rather than of what men have said in controversy over what the New Testament teaches. A basic principle of approach will be that biblical exegesis must control biblical theology and not the reverse.

[2] The kingdom of God (or heaven) is not embraced by this work for several reasons. The limitation of space is one. The limitation of purpose is another. There is a sense in which the kingdom of God has eschatological significance, but the idea is far too comprehensive to be limited to eschatology. This writer holds to the view which might be called "inaugurated eschatology": (1) Christ inaugurated the kingdom in the days of his earthly ministry; he started his spiritual reign in the hearts of the believers. (2) That which he began is destined to experience growth, both in the believer and in society; the kingdom is never static. (3) That which he started will experience a consummation in his second coming. It is in this third sense that the kingdom is an eschatological subject.

1.

Death

WITH GLOOMY FACE and grasping hands death has stalked his prey from the beginning of man's recorded history. This aspect of man's experience entered the world with a note of tragedy, as brother enraged against brother arose to kill. Since that introduction death has held men in fear of its power.

The Old Testament concept of death is marked by that which is dark and foreboding. In a day of violence men in tribal warfare watched their fellow men fall into the clutches of death by crude and cruel ways. There are places in the Old Testament where men recognized the existence of life after death. These instances are relatively few in number, and the hope they present is rather dim.

Only rarely does one rise to the height of the psalmist, "I will fear no evil . . . I will dwell in the house of the Lord for ever" or of Job, "I know that my Redeemer lives . . . and after my skin has been destroyed, yet apart from my flesh will I see God, whom I shall see for myself, and my eyes shall behold, and not another" (19:25–27),[1] or of the hope voiced in

[1] The reader's attention is directed to the fact that there is great division of opinion on the translation of this passage.

5

Daniel, "And many of those who sleep in the land of dust will awake, some to everlasting life, and some to shame and everlasting contempt" (12:2). Because of this uncertainty, death was the dread enemy of all. Death cut man off from the enjoyment of this life and delivered his body to decay. Naturally the experience was filled with fear.

The commonly accepted view of death in New Testament days was little different. For the most part people were still slaves to their fear of death. Word pictures give graphic insight into the mourning which was customary when death visited a home. Observe this in the weeping over the death of Lazarus (John 11:19 ff.) and the daughter of Jairus (Mark 5:38). The people had found little in their religion to take away this dread and fear.

It will be found that the teachings of the New Testament effect a different result. Because of Jesus' view of death and because of what his death means for those who link themselves to him by faith, death comes to lose its fearsome aspect. It is never entirely welcome when it appears, but it has lost its power to enslave man by fear. The Christian view of death is ideally founded upon the teachings of Jesus and those who followed him.

A Definition of Death

In general usage death means the cessation of life in any form. When applied to human beings, it means the cessation of life; in this experience the spirit is separated from the body. The Greek term θάνατος, translated "death," means merely "the separation (whether natural or violent) of the soul from the body by which the life on earth is ended." [2] While Thayer uses "soul," which is also widely used by others, the word "spirit" might be better. The word "soul" sometimes refers to

[2] J. H. Thayer, *A Greek-English Lexicon of the New Testament* (New York: American Book Company, 1889), p. 282.

6

the entire animated person in the sense that "I am a soul" rather than "I have a soul." At other times "soul" and "spirit" seem to be interchangeable.

Several Scripture passages illustrate the truth of this definition. James wrote, "The body apart from the spirit is dead" (2:26). Peter realized the nearness of death and described it as the "putting off" of his "tabernacle" (2 Peter 1:14–15), i.e., the spirit lays aside the physical body because it has served its purpose. When Jesus faced death on the cross, he said, "Father, into your hands I commend my spirit . . . and he yielded up his spirit" (Mark 15:37; Matt. 27:50; Luke 23:46).

This idea is also presented in the story of the rich fool (Luke 12:16–20). He had harvested an abundant crop. He had constructed barns adequate to store it all and said to his soul, "You have much goods stored up for many years; take your ease, eat, drink, and be merry." But God said to him, "Fool, this night your soul shall be required of you." When his spirit was called from his body, the life of the body ceased and the "much goods" was of no use to him. Death brings cessation of bodily activity.

One question that is frequently asked is "What happens to body and spirit at death?" Although there is no full discussion of this problem in the New Testament, there are some passages which give some light. It appears to be clear that when death comes, the body begins the process of decomposition which is natural for it. Customarily we say the body returns to the earth from which it came. It has served the need which the spirit had for it and, having served that need, is laid aside.

What happens to the spirit at death? This is the question which is not so easy to answer. Some help is given in the story which Jesus told of the rich man and the beggar, Lazarus (Luke 16:19–31). In the story the experience and destiny of two men are contrasted. The beggar, though despised in this life, died and entered immediately into a state of blessedness which is described in the statement that he was "in Abraham's bosom." The rich man, although he had every material good in this life, died and entered immediately into a state of misery.

It should be noted that as Jesus told the story he pictured the two as entering immediately into the respective states of blessedness and punishment. This suggests that at death the body of the believer returns to the earth, but his spirit enters immediately into a state of conscious blessedness. Likewise, at death the body of the unbeliever returns to the earth but his spirit enters immediately into a state of conscious punishment. This conclusion by no means solves the entire problem, but it is one part of the answer to the question.[3]

This state, separation of the spirit from the body, is not to be regarded as the final state. In subsequent chapters other phases of the problem will be presented. For the present it is sufficient to note that death means the separation of the spirit from the body, bringing to an end life and activity on this material plane.

Jesus' View of Death

Jesus' view of death was revolutionary. He referred to death as sleep. On the occasion of the raising of the daughter of Jairus, he said regarding her, "She is not dead, but sleeps" (Mark 5:39; Matt. 9:24; Luke 8:52). The people in the home,

---

[3] We should not become so involved in this aspect of the story that we forget Jesus' main point. Note (v. 14) that he was talking to men who were lovers of money. They thought a man's material status was an indication of his spiritual status. A man destitute of material goods was regarded as one upon whom God frowned; one who had great wealth was regarded as one who had God's favor. Jesus did not agree. He told this story to illustrate the fact that some men who have nothing in this world are right with God while others who have everything in this world find their eternal state in hell. The teachings of the passage on life after death and its nature are incidental. They are, nevertheless, real and important.

who had already convinced themselves that the girl was dead, laughed at him. They thought he did not know what he was talking about. They did not understand that by "sleep" he meant the ceasing of activity of this life which others call "death."

Jesus used the same idea in speaking of Lazarus, the brother of Mary and Martha. To his disciples he said, "Lazarus has fallen asleep and I go to awake him" (John 11:11). The people of Jesus' day regarded sleep during serious illness as a good sign; the patient would awake free of fever. The disciples asked why they should go merely because Lazarus was asleep. Then Jesus said to them in terms they could understand, "Lazarus is dead."

This view of death as sleep carries nothing of the current idea of "soul sleep." Jesus was presenting to the people his conception of death as something which brought quiet and rest rather than something which was to be feared as a great enemy. His other teachings indicate that he did not think of death as the unconscious existence of the spirit. His language was metaphorical for the purpose of setting out his views. Others after him used the same idea.

Jesus regarded death as having secondary importance; he made the fact of death secondary to more important matters —those pertaining to a man's duty to the will and work of God. He never looked upon death as unimportant. It is as much a part of life as birth. By the one, physical life begins; by the other, physical life ends.

Death, however, is secondary to other things. An illustration is seen in Matthew 8:21–22. Jesus called a man to come and follow him. The man agreed on the condition that he be permitted to go and bury his father. Jesus gave the rather strange command, "Follow me and let the dead bury their dead." To the twentieth-century mind this answer is very abrupt. But there is no indication that the man's father was dead or even in poor health! The man was clinging to the custom of filial devotion as a means of putting off Jesus' call to service. In essence Jesus told him to leave secondary things to people who could handle them adequately and to put his mind on the one supreme thing—his duty to God. Matters related to death are secondary to that.

The agony of Jesus in Gethsemane should not be taken as representative of his view of death or his attitude toward his own death. It is true that he shrank from the experience of death which he knew was before him. But it was not merely death from which he shrank. It was the type of death—death on the cross under the burden of the sins of the world.

No words can describe adequately the agony of a Roman crucifixion. Added to that agony was the public shame of the condemned one as his clothes were stripped from him and he was held up to public staring and mockery. To that must be added the agony of the sensitive soul of this One who had committed no sin but was suffering as though he had committed all the sins of the world.

He had told his disciples that they would all forsake him and leave him alone, but he said, "I am not alone, because the Father is with me" (John 16:32). When the awful agony of that hour came, however, he had the consciousness of being forsaken of God, and he cried, "My God, my God, why have you forsaken me?" (Matt. 27:46). The particle translated "why" is not causal, i.e., "for what *cause* have you forsaken me?" It is telic (ἴνα τι), i.e., "for what *purpose* have you forsaken me—what is to be the end of such an experience?" It was death in these circumstances which caused Jesus' agony in Gethsemane, not simply the physical aspect of death.

Paul's Teaching Regarding Death

Just as much of the best interpretation of Christian truth in other subjects is given by Paul, so in the study of death

10

he makes his splendid contribution. He used Jesus' terminology in referring to death as sleep. In 1 Thessalonians 4:13 he declared that "those who have fallen asleep" will experience all the glory of the Lord's return. In Acts 7:60 the death of Stephen is described in the expression "he fell asleep." The entire account bears the marks of an eyewitness. It is not at all improbable that Luke got the story from Paul, who was present at the stoning of Stephen.

In Paul's teaching, as in that of Jesus, there is no element of "soul sleep" involved. Departure from this life means presence and fellowship with the Lord. "Sleep" is merely a metaphorical way of speaking of death.

In Paul's view death was introduced into the world by sin and is universal in scope (Rom. 5:12 ff.). The reign of death he saw as an indication of the reign of sin from the time of Adam. Adam sinned against direct prohibitive law— "You shall not." After the giving of the law through Moses, men again sinned against direct prohibitive law— "You shall not." From Adam to Moses there was no direct prohibitive law. There were, however, eternal principles upon which law was later built. Men sinned against these principles.

As Paul saw it, the presence of death during all that time was an indication of sin even though there was no direct law against which men sinned. Paul made a direct relation between sin and death as the penalty for sin. It appears that he looked on death as the penalty of original sin for the unbeliever, but for the believer the idea of penalty is lost and death becomes a means of entrance into blessedness with God.

It is true that wherever the Scriptures speak of death as the penalty for sin the main emphasis is on spiritual death, i.e., separation from the blessings and fellowship of God. Physical death, however, cannot be removed from the picture entirely. In Paul's view the two, sin and death, entered the world together. They reign together in universal scope. The time is coming, however, when both shall be completely subjugated to the power of Christ. He conquered death and sin by his death and resurrection. In regeneration and resurrection the believer, too, is to gain complete victory over sin and death. Men lose much through their relationship to Adam; they gain infinitely more through their relationship to Christ.

According to Paul, the body is subject to death but the spirit is not (Rom. 8:10), and in God's own time the body is to be so transformed that it can never be subject to death again. This naturally presents the much discussed problem of whether man was created mortal or immortal. That is, was he created immortal but became mortal when he sinned? Or was he subject to death from the beginning? Paul offered no answer to the problem. He did indicate in 1 Corinthians 15:50–53 that the type of body which men have is not fit for eternal habitation due to its mortal nature. It must be changed if it is to be fit for the spirit's eternal dwelling.

Jesus has abolished death (2 Tim. 1:10) and has brought forth life and immortality. In the purpose of God, Jesus has already abolished death; in reality, that act is not yet consummated. It will be perfected in the resurrection, when men are changed so they can never die. The writer of the Epistle to the Hebrews had a similar concept of Jesus' work: "that through death he might break the power of the one having the power of death, that is, the devil" (Heb. 2:14–15). Because of the relation of sin and death the devil has used death as a club to bring fear to men. Through his redemptive death Jesus has wrested this club from the devil, and death holds no fear for those who have found in Christ redemption from sin and death.

Paul faced his own death with mingled emotions. In Philippians 1:21–23 he expressed the idea that to die means to depart from this life and be with Christ. That for Paul was much better than to continue to live in the midst of the hardships which were his in his missionary work. Philippians was written while Paul was a prisoner, awaiting trial before Caesar. His first impression was that to depart from this life and be with Christ was much more to be desired than imprisonment.

It should be noted that this attitude was due in no way to the Greek concept that the body was evil and that the spirit could have no freedom until it was free of the body.[4] This was not Paul's view. His view was related only to the extreme hardship which had been his for several years and which made departure from this life attractive. At the same time, however, he felt that he could be of further service to the Philippians by continuing in this life and was rather certain in his heart that that was to be the case.

Paul also believed that departing this life is not entirely a pleasant prospect (2 Cor. 5:1–10). This passage will be given full consideration in chapter 3. For the present purpose it is sufficient to see that Paul shrank somewhat from what he saw before him. He knew that God gave a body to his spirit for this life. He knew that God would give a body to his spirit for the next life. He knew that that body would be given at the resurrection of the dead (1 Cor. 15).

He saw, then, that to depart from this life was for the spirit to lay aside the body and become a disembodied spirit until the eternal body is given. Paul did not anticipate with pleasure becoming a disembodied spirit. He wished that he might put on his eternal body over this temporal body and thus escape death. He was willing, however, to depart from this life and become temporarily a disembodied spirit because to be absent from the body is to be at home with the Lord.

In 2 Timothy 4:6–8 Paul saw death as the crowning event of a well-spent life of service to God. He had been a good soldier—"fought a good fight." He had been a successful ath-

[4] Cf. Emil Brunner, *Man in Revolt* (Philadelphia: The Westminster Press, 1947), pp. 374–75.

lete—"finished the course." He had been a good preacher—
"kept the faith." All that was behind; death was before him as
he was about to be "poured out as a drink offering upon God's
altar." He saw pleasant prospect ahead because there was reserved for him the reward reserved for all those who love
Christ. Death was not defeat; it was glorious victory. He would
have agreed with the much later statement in Revelation 14:13
of the strangest beatitude: "Blessed are the dead which die
in the Lord."

2.

The Disembodied State

THIS CHAPTER must begin with a discussion of terms. Indeed, for many it should begin with one huge question mark! Objective observation regarding life does not extend beyond the grave; reason, faith, and the Scriptures speak of survival and of resurrection. The field of investigation and speculation, then, is left open. Various approaches have been made to the problem of the nature of the soul's existence between death and the resurrection.

One approach is that represented by Owen.[1] He rejects life of any kind between death and resurrection due to his view of the nature of man. He rejects as false a scientific naturalism which would find in man no spirit nature or life other than the natural and material existence. He rejects as equally false what he calls the traditional religious view of man: he is made up of physical body and soul and the soul can live after the death of the body. He argues that this idea was adapted from Greek thought; it has no place in the main stream of Christian belief, which grew out of Hebrew religion and not Greek

---

[1] D. R. G. Owen, *Body and Soul* (Philadelphia: The Westminster Press, 1956). See also Brunner, *op. cit.*, pp. 362–89, 462–77, for a better discussion of the "unified nature of man" view.

philosophy. He grants a few instances in the New Testament which appear to present this view, but he holds that they have slipped in and do not belong in the main stream of Christian thought.

Examination of the New Testament, however, fails to reveal any such idea. When Paul looked upon death as desirable,[2] it was not due to such a disparaging view of the evil nature of the body. The setting was one in which the Apostle contrasted the almost indescribably difficult life of suffering in his missionary work with the glorious prospect of the immediate presence and fellowship of Christ which would be his at death.

Owen holds that the Hebrew view of man was that of an animated body. The soul or spirit is only this body as animated, as active. When the body dies the soul dies, too. Soul and body live together; they perish together. Owen believes that God's purpose for man will be seen in the resurrection, when the total man, body-soul, will be raised from death. He recognizes that this view will hold difficulty for those who wish to know about this interim between the death of the body-soul and the resurrection of the body-soul "at the last day." However, since the Bible tells us very little about what happens after death, in the final consummation, or of God's ultimate purpose for man, theologians should admit that they know nothing. His argument for a resurrection but his denial of an interval between the death of the body-soul and "the last day" is not clear.

In appraisal of Owen's position it should be observed that his argument is not convincing due to the fact that he omits large parts of the total picture. What he calls exposition of the Scriptures is the weakest part of the work; it is not exposition in the accepted use of the term. The position which he sets out is not biblical, it is not "orthodox" in the sense of Protes-

---

[2] See the discussion on page 12 ff. See also Anders Nygren, *Commentary on Romans* (Philadelphia: Muhlenberg Press, 1949), p. 333.

tant orthodoxy,[3] and it is one which attacks scientific naturalism not so much as it does basic supernaturalism. His view will not stand the test of exegesis.

When Owen's entire argument has been examined, there is still another question: has all truth come from the Hebrews? Has none come from other cultures? Further, what of the matter of Christian doctrine in relation to Hebrew theology? At many places Christian theology goes far beyond Hebrew theology. Does it not do the same where eschatology is concerned? Surely God's continuing revelation has some word to speak here.

Still another approach to the nature of man's experience between death and resurrection is that represented by Chafer.[4] This is the view that the believer is at the point of death given an intermediate body so that he will not be bodiless between giving up the natural body in death and receiving the spiritual body at the resurrection. The basis for this belief is reluctance to accept the idea of the spirit's having life apart from the body; the scriptural background which Chafer cites is 2 Corinthians 5:1–4. This intermediate body is "from heaven." Its being from heaven does not require that it be used forever. It will be exchanged for the eternal body at the time of the resurrection.

This view is foreign to the New Testament unless this is the correct interpretation of 2 Corinthians 5:1–4. Chafer's interpretation is not the almost universally accepted one, as will be seen in the exegesis of the passage later in this chapter and in chapter 3.

Yet another view of man's experience between death and the resurrection is that based upon statements from Martin

[3] That is, it is not the view set out in the confessions of faith of the various non–Roman Catholic groups.

[4] Lewis Sperry Chafer, *Major Bible Themes* (Chicago: Moody Press, 1926), p. 304, and *Systematic Theology* (Dallas: Dallas Seminary Press, 1948), II, 156; VII, 56, 202.

Luther.[5] This view is that the interval is like the experience of sleep: one goes to sleep, and after a few hours of sleep he awakes without consciousness of time lapse and without consciousness of what has happened to him in the interim of sleep. So Luther held that the righteous dead will sleep until the Lord comes to knock on the grave and bid them wake up. The first righteous man who ever died will arise on the last day and think he has slept scarcely an hour. There seems to be an inconsistency between this and Luther's view, expressed elsewhere, that after death souls hear, see, and perceive but those yet alive cannot know how they do so.[6] Calvin did not accept the view of sleep without consciousness; he called it frenzy and those who held to it fanatics.[7] It is his view that the souls of the righteous dead live and enjoy quiet rest but that the whole of their felicity is to be experienced only in the resurrection.

The term "disembodied" is not the usual one for a study of this phase of eschatology. The customary term is "intermediate," a term accurately used insofar as it describes a state which is between the natural body before death and the spiritual body after the resurrection. It is purposely avoided in this treatment because of the suggestion that the state described is something of a halfway ground between one state and another. In a sense, perhaps, that is true, but the term has led to unfortunate inductions and suggestions on the part of those who have considered it.

The eternal state is to be a bodily state (spiritual body) just as the present state is a bodily state (physical body). The term "disembodied" is used to describe that state of spiritual

[5] Martin Luther, *Luthers Werke* (Berlin: C. V. Schwetschke und Sohn, 1898), I, 40, 57, 75; Hugh Thomson Kerr (ed.), *A Compend of Luther's Theology* (Philadelphia: The Westminster Press, 1943), pp. 238, 242.

[6] Luther, *op. cit.*, p. 241.

[7] John Calvin, *Commentary on the Epistles of Paul to the Corinthians* (Grand Rapids: Wm. B. Eerdmans Publishing Co., 1948), II, 20–21.

18

existence which the individual experiences in the interim between his death and his resurrection. Comparison of the two terms will reveal that "disembodied" is better than "intermediate" as a description of that state.

The term "state" has been used all through the history of Christian doctrine. It is considered a better descriptive term than "place" for two reasons. It avoids the idea of material which is associated with the word "place" without taking away any of the reality of being. Then, too, it avoids the suggestion of a "halfway house" between this world and the eternal one.

By "disembodied state," then, is meant *the conscious existence of both the righteous and the wicked after death and prior to the resurrection.* The New Testament affirms such a state. In this state the spirit is without a body, yet for the righteous it is a state of conscious joy and blessedness, while for the wicked it is a state of conscious suffering.

It must be granted that the New Testament references to such a state are not numerous. They are, however, clear and sufficient when considered in the light of Scripture references on other subjects. We do well to look through the windows that are available, however small they may be. They neither solve all the problems nor give all the answers to curious minds, however sincere.

This disembodied state may be recognized by implication, but implication that is inescapable, on the basis of the Scriptures which have to do with death and the resurrection. The New Testament teaches that at death the body returns to the earth, and the spirit enters into a state of conscious existence either in blessedness or suffering. The New Testament also teaches that the body will be raised and transformed at the resurrection when Christ returns to the earth. If these two propositions are taught in the New Testament, it follows that there is a disembodied state of conscious existence of the spirit between the two events, death and resurrection. Some type of life or existence in this interim is theologically inescapable.[8] What is the nature of that state? It seems wise to divide the answer to the question, considering first the passages relating to the righteous and then those relating to the unrighteous.

The Righteous

It has been observed in the previous chapter that at death bodily activity ceases and the body begins the process of decay which is inherent in its nature. It has also been observed that the spirit enters into a conscious state of existence. It is the nature of this state which must now be studied.

With God.—The disembodied righteous are with God. The statement of Ecclesiastes 12:7 that the spirit returns to God who gave it finds repetition in New Testament passages. In Philippians 1:23 Paul spoke of departing to be with Christ. He was referring to his dilemma as he faced the prospect of death. He realized that to continue this life meant much hardship, but to close this life meant departure to the immediate presence of Christ.

The same idea is voiced in 2 Corinthians 5:8, where Paul spoke of being away from the body and at home with the Lord. He understood that at death he would give up his bodily existence and enter into the immediate presence of the Lord. This passage will be discussed at length in chapter 3. For present purposes it is sufficient to see its reflection of Paul's assurance that not even death could separate him from his Lord.

In Luke 23:43 Jesus assured the penitent thief, "Today you will be with me in paradise." In Luke 16:22 the expression "carried to Abraham's bosom" is clearly a descriptive term

[8] T. A. Kantonen, *The Christian Hope* (Philadelphia: Muhlenberg Press, 1954), pp. 36–48; Oscar Cullmann, *Christ and Time* (London: Student Christian Movement Press, Ltd., 1952), pp. 231–343.

referring to the state of blessedness in the presence of God. No greater joy could be contemplated by a good Hebrew than to be clasped to the bosom of Abraham, the father of the race.

Paul in 1 Thessalonians 4:14 stated in connection with the Lord's return that God will bring with him (Christ) those who have fallen asleep. Many other implications are to be found in these passages, but the emphasis here is that the righteous enter immediately at death into the presence of God.

In Paradise.—The disembodied righteous are in paradise. The word "paradise" is a transliteration of the Greek word παράδεισος. Most authorities hold that the word is of Persian origin; some suggest an Armenian origin. In every nonbiblical usage it refers to a garden or park, a place of beauty and enjoyment. The Septuagint translators used the term to represent the garden of Eden in Genesis 2:8. The earliest record of the word in Greek indicates a garden. This same connotation is found in numerous references in nonbiblical papyri.

The word is found three times in the New Testament. In Luke 23:43 Jesus assured the penitent thief, "Today you will be with me in paradise." Wherever Jesus went at death, the thief went with him. The term "paradise" is used to describe that blessed experience. In 2 Corinthians 12:4 Paul described an experience in which he was "caught up into paradise." No other indication of the place is given unless the term "paradise" is to be understood as a parallel to "the third heaven" in verse 2. Wherever it was, it afforded Paul an experience by way of revelation. The things he experienced were of such exalted nature that he was not permitted to make them known to men.

In Revelation 2:7 the one who overcomes is assured that the living Christ will grant him the privilege of eating of the tree of life "which is in the paradise of God." Although the term "paradise" is not used in Revelation 22:1–2, it is likely that the idea is the same. In this passage the tree of life is seen beside the river of the water of life, and the total picture is of a paradise or garden.

These references appear to indicate that paradise is where God dwells. It needs to be positionized no further than that. The indication is, too, that at death the righteous go immediately to be with God in paradise—into a state of blessedness in God's presence.

Alive and conscious.—The disembodied righteous are alive and conscious. While the New Testament teaches a disembodied state during the interim between death and the resurrection, it nowhere leaves the idea that this is a state of suspended animation or of unconsciousness. Several passages aid in understanding this point.

In Matthew 22:32 Jesus told the Sadducees that God is the God of the living. His statement was made in reference to the words addressed to Moses at the burning bush, "I am the God of Abraham, Isaac, and Jacob." Jesus interpreted the statement to mean that God was saying, "Abraham, Isaac, and Jacob died long ago, but they are still alive." There is no indication that a state of unconsciousness was meant.

Jesus said, in John 11:26, "Whoever lives and believes in me will never die." He was not speaking of the experience of physical death. He was saying that physical death did not bring about a cessation of conscious existence and fellowship with Christ. Likewise, in Luke 16:22–23 Jesus represented Lazarus as alive and conscious "in Abraham's bosom" immediately after death.

Paul in Philippians 1:23 found this disembodied state to be a far better one than the bodily state which he was experiencing at the time. His mind flashed back over the years of his missionary travel. That travel had resulted in arrest and years of imprisonment in Jerusalem, Caesarea, and Rome. As he wrote from his prison in Rome, he considered the two

22

prospects before him. Release from prison meant further service of the type previously experienced. Death meant the cessation of the hardship of this life and entrance into the immediate presence and fellowship of his Lord. Of the two, Paul found the second to be far better. It is extremely doubtful that he would have felt this way about it had he looked upon it as a state of unconsciousness. To see it, however, as a state of conscious existence in the presence of the Lord was a glorious prospect.

At rest.—The disembodied righteous are at rest. This statement is based on the words of Revelation 14:13, "Blessed are the dead who die in the Lord henceforth. 'Blessed indeed,' says the Spirit, 'that they may rest from their labors, for their deeds follow them.'" The idea involved in the term "rest" is that of being refreshed after toil. Those who die in the Lord are described as being in a blessed state because they enter upon an experience of enjoyment as they are refreshed after the toil of this life. More than that, their work does not stop when they die. It keeps working effectively to that day when the books shall be opened (Rev. 20:12).

Conclusions

Before taking up the New Testament passages relative to the disembodied wicked it may be found helpful to summarize the above discussion by stating some conclusions.

A conscious state.—There is no basis in the New Testament for what is known as a condition of soul sleep. Those who hold to that view hold that the spirits of the dead remain in a state of unconsciousness until the resurrection of the body, at which time spirit and body are reunited and consciousness returns. While the New Testament refers to death as "sleep," it does not refer to soul sleep. The term "sleep" is used as a metaphorical description of the cessation of bodily activity at death. In fact, there is one passage (1 Thess. 5:10) in which death is

23

spoken of as sleep and at the same time conscious fellowship with Christ is indicated: "that whether we wake or *sleep* we might *live with him.*"

A fixed state.—The moral and spiritual quality of an individual is a decided matter at death. This quality is determined by an individual's reaction to God and God's offer of mercy and forgiveness. This reaction is a matter of activity in this life rather than in life after physical death. There is no New Testament basis for the idea of a second chance after death or a purgatorial cleansing which would alter the spiritual quality which one possessed at death.

An incomplete state.—While this is a conscious state and one in which the spiritual quality of the individual is fixed, it is not looked upon as the final state. Paul shrank from it and wished that he could "put on" his eternal body over this mortal one and thus by-pass the disembodied state (2 Cor. 5:3–4). He saw the disembodied state before him but longed for the resurrection (Phil. 3:10–11). All the New Testament regards the final state as coming with the resurrection. Man in his total personality is body as well as spirit. Hence the disembodied state is necessarily lacking in one element of human perfection; this part will be supplied at the resurrection.

The Wicked

New Testament passages concerning the disembodied state of the wicked are even fewer in number than those relating to the righteous. The few which relate to this topic lead to several conclusions.

Separate from God.—The disembodied wicked are separated from God. This idea is suggested by the account of Lazarus and the rich man in Luke 16:23. Immediately after death Lazarus was carried to the bosom of Abraham, a metaphorical expression of the presence of God. The rich man, on the contrary, was found to be removed from Abraham and Lazarus immediately after death with an impassable gulf separating them. All the blessings of Lazarus in the presence of God were denied the rich man in this separation.

The term "separated from God" in no way suggests conflict with the concept of God's omnipresence. The idea is that of separation from the blessings and fellowship of God. In his picture of judgment in the "sheep and goat" passage (Matt. 25:31–46) Jesus used such terms as *"depart from me . . . into everlasting fire"* and "these *will go away* into everlasting punishment." Whatever idea of separation is meant in this relationship is that which is meant in the use of the term "separated from God."

Alive and conscious.—The disembodied wicked are alive and conscious. In the above account the rich man is represented as being alive and conscious of his surroundings. He was aware of his condition; he was aware of suffering; he was aware of the desirability of warning his brothers who were yet alive and able to escape his fate.

Punishment.—The disembodied wicked are suffering punishment. This was true of the rich man. He died and found himself immediately in a state of torment. The intensity of his suffering is reflected in his request for the comforting ministry of Lazarus and his desire that his brothers escape that fate.

An additional idea is found in 2 Peter 2:9. There the implication is that the Lord knows how to keep the unrighteous under punishment until the day of judgment. This indicates that the unrighteous enter immediately into a state of punishment and that they experience that punishment to the time of final judgment. Their fate at that time will be discussed in the chapter on eternal destiny.

First Peter 3:19–20 is frequently used in the treatment of the teaching on the disembodied wicked. The passage is of highly controversial nature and of questionable value in such a study as this. Where did Jesus go at death?

25

The answer depends in part at least on the Greek participle in verse 20 which is translated "disobedient." The participle has no article and in general usage would not be translated "who were disobedient" but instead "when they were disobedient." In this usage it would refer to the witnessing of the eternal Spirit at the time of the disobedience in the days of Noah. Every blow of Noah's hammer was a voice witnessing to the judgment of God that was about to fall on men who went on heedlessly in their wickedness. Imprisoned by sin in the time of their sin and rejection, they continued to be "imprisoned spirits."

The emphasis of the passage would be that Jesus was raised up in the power of that same eternal Spirit which was operative even back in the time of Noah. This view has had its adherents throughout the period of Christian interpretation—Augustine, Bede, Aquinas, Lyra, Hammond, Beza, Scholinger, Hornius, Gerhard, Hofmann, Doddridge, Wichelhaus, Besser, Scott, Benson, Clausen, Pearson, and Williams.

There have been many interpretations of the passage from the opposing view: that between his death and his resurrection Jesus preached to the wicked dead. The most comprehensive statement of these views is set out by Reicke.[9] He surveys many views but endorses the view that Jesus went to proclaim his lordship over even the wicked dead. One thing is clear; so controversial a passage cannot be definitive where the disembodied state is being discussed.

At a fixed place.—What is to be said of the "place" where the disembodied wicked undergo this imprisonment and punishment? The New Testament is not as clear on this subject as it is in the case of the disembodied righteous, who are spoken of as entering paradise. The only term used in the New Testament that would serve as a parallel in the experience of

[9] Bo Reicke, *The Disobedient Spirits and Christian Baptism* (Copenhagen: Ejnar Munksgaard, 1946).

the wicked is the word "Hades." In Luke 16:23 the rich man is described as being in Hades. It is easy to say that this passage settles the matter and indicates that the wicked dead are in Hades. Such an easy solution, however, cannot be altogether satisfactory.

The term "Hades" ('Άιδης) is derived from the infinitive ἰδεῖν, "to see," and the alpha privative which makes the idea negative, "not to see." Hades, then, means the *unseen* world as compared to this *visible* one. It meant for those who first used it the unseen world inhabited by the spirits of dead men—good or bad. The ancient pagan writers divided Hades into two parts: Elysium, the abode of the righteous, and Tartarus, the abode of the wicked.

The translators of the Septuagint used Hades to translate the Hebrew "Sheol," a word meaning "the grave." Generally no distinction was made between righteous and wicked. They were spoken of as entering Hades, the region of the dead, at the time of death.

The term "Hades" is used eleven times in the New Testament:

(1) Matthew 11:23; Luke 10:15—Capernaum was to be brought down to Hades because she rejected the offer of God's mercy extended through his Son. She was compared to Sodom, which was brought to death—destruction—because of her wickedness.

(2) Matthew 16:18—The gates of Hades will not be able to withstand the attack made by the church.

(3) Luke 16:23—In Hades the rich man lifted up his eyes.

(4) Acts 2:27—The psalmist believed that God would not leave his soul in Hades.

(5) Acts 2:31—This is Peter's statement of his assurance that God did not leave the soul of his Son in Hades nor permit his holy One to experience decay.

(6) 1 Corinthians 15:55—"O death, where is your victory?

27

O Hades, where is your sting?" Many ancient manuscripts do not use "Hades" in this passage, repeating θάνατε, "death," instead, "O death, where is your victory? O death, where is your sting?" Such usage indicates that death and Hades were synonymous in the thinking of many.

(7) Revelation 1:18—Jesus the risen Christ has the key to death and Hades.

(8) Revelation 6:8—Death and Hades follow the rider on the pale (corpse-colored) horse.

(9) Revelation 20:13–14—Death and Hades deliver up the dead that were in them. Then they are cast into the lake of fire.

Careful analysis of the above passages will indicate that Hades seems to be used in the following ways:

(1) As a general reference to the grave—Acts 2:27, 31; 1 Corinthians 15:55; Revelation 1:18; 6:8.

(2) As a specific reference to the place of the departed wicked—Luke 16:23; Revelation 20:14.

(3) As a general reference to death or extinction, or as a specific reference with the evil sense of "hell" implied—Matthew 11:23; Luke 10:15; Matthew 16:18; Revelation 20:13. These passages may be interpreted as general or specific according to the context.

It appears, then, that we cannot say that the disembodied wicked are in Hades and have the matter settled as easily as we do when we say that the disembodied righteous are in paradise. We can only say that they are kept under punishment. The term "Gehenna," "hell," which always bears an evil connotation, will be discussed in the chapter on eternal destiny. At this point we can view the wicked only immediately beyond death.

Conclusions

It is possible to reach some conclusions concerning the state of the disembodied wicked.

A conscious state.—Review of the passages discussed will make this clear.

A fixed state.—The rich man was told clearly that his state was one which was fixed and which could not be changed to a better one.

An incomplete state.—Those in this state are conscious; they have begun to endure the penalty of their wicked lives; this penalty will be consummated in the experience of the resurrection and final judgment. It should be observed carefully that here, as in the case of the disembodied righteous, there is no basis for belief in any form of purgatorial cleansing through suffering so as to prepare the individual for a better state. Apocatastasis of this type is foreign to the text of the New Testament.[10]

[10] Those interested in further study of the subject and viewpoint treated in this chapter will find great profit in such standard theological works as: A. A. Hodge, *Outlines of Theology* (New York: Robert Carter and Brothers, 1882); Edgar Young Mullins, *The Christian Religion in Its Doctrinal Expression* (Philadelphia: Judson Press, 1938); Augustus Hopkins Strong, *Systematic Theology* (Philadelphia: Judson Press, 1942).

3.

The Resurrection

THE IDEA of survival beyond death is common to many of the world's living religions. Even a casual reading in the field of comparative religion will indicate that this is true. Such casual reading will indicate, too, that the variations on that theme are numerous. The ideas of future survival range all the way from the mystical reabsorption into the Infinite of philosophic Hinduism to the Mohammedan's belief in a sensuous existence in the garden of Allah, where men will be married to "large-eyed maids" and shall drink of a flowing wine which will cause neither headaches nor dimmed wits. Between these extremes are found manifold views of the nature of life after death.

Because of this variety of ideas it is necessary to preface the present study with a definition of the word "resurrection." The English word is derived directly from the Latin *resurrectio,* which is parallel to the Greek ἀνάστασις. This Greek noun is derived from the verb ἴστημι meaning "to stand" or "to cause to stand," plus the preposition ἀνά meaning "up" or "again." The noun, then, means a state of standing up or a state of standing again, i.e., re-standing. The English verb "rise" or "raise" may be used, "to rise up" or "to be raised up."

In New Testament usage, wherever the word relates to the body, it means the raising up of the body, the return of the body from the clutches of death. Any view of future survival which leaves out this restoration of the body from death back to life cannot be spoken of as a resurrection in the New Testament meaning of the term. Such views may describe a condition of life beyond death, but they are not in line with the New Testament connotation of resurrection. In the present study, then, the term "resurrection" is used to mean *the raising up of the body so that it is released from the powers of death and made to live, to stand up again.* The quality of this body or life will be a part of the discussion. It should be noted in the beginning, however, that the New Testament doctrine of the resurrection is *not* a doctrine of mere resuscitation, i.e., a restoration to the physical functions of this life such as was experienced by Lazarus, the daughter of Jairus, the son of the widow at Nain, etc. That it is far from that will become evident in the discussion.

The doctrine of the resurrection was much discussed in the day of Jesus and the apostles. Some reflections of its importance are to be found in the Old Testament. There was a marked development of man's understanding of the resurrection during the intertestamental period as the circumstances of life turned the minds of men from national welfare and existence to individual welfare and existence in relationship to God, i.e., to personal destiny rather than national destiny.

It is in the New Testament that the doctrine is stated in climactic form. Reflections of belief in the life of the body after death are seen in the view that Jesus was John the Baptist made alive again (Mark 6:16; Matt. 14:2; Luke 9:7). This, however, is a very distorted view which is more in line with resuscitation or even transmigration. A better statement of belief in the resurrection is that voiced by Martha when, on the occasion of her brother's death, she said, "I know that he will

31

rise again in the resurrection at the last day" (John 11:24). The doctrine was a favorite point of debate between the Pharisees, who accepted it, and the Sadducees, who rejected it. Their disputes are frequently mentioned in the New Testament.

The Resurrection of Jesus

Logically the New Testament doctrine of the resurrection must be presented in two phases—the resurrection of Jesus and the resurrection of others. Paul and his contemporaries who were interpreters of the Christian religion based their doctrine of the resurrection on the resurrection of Jesus; whatever he experienced in being raised from death in God's time and purpose will happen to others. The present study will follow that development.

Jesus' prediction.—Jesus predicted his own resurrection. This is the first evidence of the doctrine in New Testament records. Jesus knew that death at the hands of his enemies awaited him in Jerusalem. He knew, too, that death could not hold him because it had no rightful claim on him; victorious over death, he would be raised from the grave. This assurance is reflected in many passages.

In Matthew 12:39–40; 16:4; and Luke 11:29 the "sign of Jonah" was offered to the scribes and Pharisees. Jesus said that as Jonah was in the belly of the whale three days and nights so would the Son of man be in the heart of the earth for a like period. This reference to his resurrection is an indication that in Jesus' thinking it was to be the greatest "sign" of his being what he claimed to be—the Anointed One of God.

In Mark 8:31; Matthew 16:21; and Luke 9:22 Jesus announced that he would be killed but raised up on the third day. The same prediction of his resurrection on the third day is recorded in Mark 9:31; 10:34; Matthew 17:23; 20:19; and Luke 18:33. Mark indicates by the use of the imperfect tense

(9:31) that Jesus taught the disciples repeatedly that he would die but that he would be raised on the third day.[1] Similarly in John 2:19 Jesus referred to his resurrection in the statement, "Destroy this temple, and in three days I will raise it up."

In Mark 9:9 and Matthew 17:9 Jesus told the disciples not to report the transfiguration until after his resurrection. In Matthew 26:32 he instructed his disciples that after his resurrection he would meet them in Galilee. In John 16:16 he said, "A little while and you will see me no more; again a little while and you will see me." He was speaking of his separation from them by death and his restoration to them by the resurrection.

Such abundance of references reveals that Jesus predicted his resurrection, that it was much in his mind, and that it was of the utmost importance in his role as the Suffering Servant Messiah.

The resurrection.—The resurrection of Jesus is a fact. The New Testament affirms that Jesus' physical body did not decay in the grave. It was made alive again, gloriously transformed so that it was no longer limited by time and space nor subject to change, decay, and death. Such an event can be accepted only on the strongest evidence, and it is doubtful that

---

[1] No difficulty should be created over the two statements that (1) Jesus would be raised *on the third day* and (2) Jesus would be in the heart of the earth *three days and nights.* At first glance there does appear to be a difficulty. If he lay in the grave three days and nights (three periods of twenty-four hours each) and then was raised, obviously he would be raised on the fourth day and not on the third. The difficulty is in our twentieth-century way of reckoning time. In the first century no difficulty was involved. Any part of a day would be spoken of as a day. This was true in Greek, Roman, and Jewish custom. In the experience of Jesus there were three periods of twenty-four hours each—by our calendar Friday, Saturday, and Sunday—involved. Jesus was crucified on Friday at 9:00 A.M., pronounced dead at 3:00 P.M., and in the grave before 6:00 P.M. He was in the grave all of Saturday and a part of Sunday. The resurrection apparently took place near sunrise on Sunday morning. By all first-century ways of reckoning time, he was in the grave three days and nights and at the same time he was raised on the third day.

any other event in the recorded life of Jesus is supported by better proof. A major place was given to it by the New Testament writers. The record of his resurrection is presented in the following Scripture passages: Matthew 28; Mark 16:1–19; Luke 24; John 20–21; Acts 1:3–8; and 1 Corinthians 15:3–7.

These passages indicate beyond question that the early Christians believed that Jesus was raised from the dead and that he appeared to his disciples. How is that belief to be explained? Reverent scholarship accepts the record at face value and holds that Jesus was raised exactly as the New Testament records the event. From the day of his recorded resurrection, however, there have been those who have denied this fact and have tried in many ways to explain the presence of the resurrection accounts in the New Testament. Several well-known theories have been presented in such explanation.[2]

Perhaps the "stolen body" theory, i.e., the idea that the disciples of Jesus stole his body and then reported that he had been raised, is the oldest. This theory was first advanced by the Jewish chief priests and later by Reimarus and others. The "swoon" theory, found in the teaching of Heinrich Paulus[3] and others, held that Jesus did not die on the cross. He swooned and was revived by the cool atmosphere of the tomb, the odor of the spices, etc.

The "wrong tomb" theory was presented by Kirsopp Lake[4] as an explanation of what may have happened. The women who went to the tomb early on Sunday morning to finish

[2] Cf. John McNaugher, *Jesus Christ, the Same Yesterday, Today, and Forever* (New York: Fleming H. Revell Co., 1947); William Milligan, *The Resurrection of Our Lord* (New York: The MacMillan Co., 1927); Doremus A. Hayes, *The Resurrection Fact* (Nashville: Cokesbury Press, 1932); Floyd E. Hamilton, *The Basis of Christian Faith* (New York: George H. Doran Co., 1927).
[3] Heinrich Eberhard Gottlob Paulus, *Das Leben Jesu* (Heidelberg: C. F. Winter, 1828), pp. 266–344.
[4] Kirsopp Lake, *The Historical Evidence for the Resurrection of Jesus Christ* (New York: G. P. Putnam's Sons, 1912), pp. 251–52.

anointing the body of Jesus were met by a young man near the place where they thought Jesus had been buried. The young man, attempting to help them, said, "You are looking for Jesus of Nazareth. He is not here. Behold the place where the Lord lay," pointing to the right tomb. The women misunderstood and went away with their report that an "angel" had told them that Jesus had been raised.

Another theory, known as the "vision" theory, has been held from the time of Strauss [5] to the present. The disciples believed so firmly that Jesus would be raised that they had visions or hallucinations that they had seen him. These reported experiences grew as they were retold until the full-grown resurrection belief swept the early Christian group.

Karl Keim [6] has presented what has been called the "telegram" theory, i.e., the spirit of Christ, living on after the death of the body, communicated with the disciples to let them know that he was still alive. By these "telegrams from heaven" the disciples became certain that Jesus lived even beyond death.

According to the "legendary" theory, represented by Weizsäcker,[7] Jesus never rose from the dead nor were there any appearances, objective or subjective. The "myth" of the resurrection grew up in the early church as believers sought to explain Jesus' personality and spiritual impact upon men. They believed that so superior a Person must have lived on after death. Such belief led gradually to the idea of the resurrection of Jesus.

Some have held to what is known as the "hyperbolic" theory, i.e., the early disciples used such a strong language in describing the continuing life of the crucified Christ that misunderstanding came into the church at an early date. Finally

[5] David Friedrick Strauss, A New Life of Jesus (London: Williams and Norgate, 1879), I, 400–404.
[6] Karl Keim, Jesus von Nazara (Publisher's data not available), pp. 279, 601.
[7] Carl von Weizsäcker, The Apostolic Age of the Christian Church, trans. James Millar (New York: G. P. Putnam's Sons, 1907), I, 7–19.

this misunderstanding was recorded in the form of the resurrection accounts.

Yet another view is that the body of Jesus was not raised from the dead at all. The empty tomb was due to a miracle of disposal by which God annihilated the physical body of Jesus so that whatever survived death was of some spirit nature only. Skrine [8] presents this idea and explains that the so-called "appearances" of Jesus were the result of the impact of the consciousness of Jesus on the consciousness of the disciples. He holds that God disposed of the body of Jesus by withdrawing it into nothingness because the disciples would not have believed that Jesus had in any way survived death if they had been able to see the body still in the grave. For Skrine the appearances are best illustrated by speaking of them as something like unusually vivid cases of thought transference between Jesus and the disciples.

These are representative of the views opposing the idea that Jesus was actually raised from the dead. Other theories have been suggested, but these are the more outstanding ones. Space cannot be given here to refutation. Worthy works previously cited point out the failure of these theories to satisfy the facts involved. One of the most helpful treatments is by McNaugher.[9]

A review of the New Testament records of the resurrection of Jesus affords a most interesting study. The similarities and differences in the separate accounts have been emphasized frequently. On the main points the records agree. They agree that the time of the resurrection was early in the morning of the first day of the week, that women came first to the tomb, that the tomb was open and empty, that the tomb was guarded by angels, that the angels announced the resurrection,

[8] John Huntley Skrine, *The Gospel of the Manhood* (London: Skeffington and Son, Ltd., 1922), pp. 65–74.
[9] McNaugher, *op. cit.*, pp. 144–60.

that the angels sent a message to the disciples, and that Jesus appeared to his disciples several times.

There are slight differences in the accounts. They differ as to the exact hour of the visit of the women—Mark: very early on the first day of the week; Matthew: after the sabbath as the first day dawned; Luke: on the first day at early dawn; John: on the first day while it was yet dark. They differ as to the names and number of the women—Mark: Mary Magdalene, Mary the mother of Jesus, Salome; Matthew: Mary Magdalene, the other Mary; Luke: "they," evidently a reference to the women from Galilee; John: Mary Magdalene. They differ as to the number of angels—Mark and Matthew: one; Luke and John: two. They differ as to the exact time and wording of the message to the disciples.

These points of difference are not contradictory; they are complementary. They also reflect the particular purpose of each writer. Matthew presents those things which afford a touch with Jewish life; Mark presents those things which arouse wonder and amazement; Luke presents those things which indicate human interest and sympathy; John presents the effect of the resurrection on particular individuals, i.e., Mary Magdalene, Peter, "that disciple whom Jesus loved," Thomas, etc. Thus the "gospel quartet" sings a marvelous story; the four sing in harmony but not in unison.

Jesus' appearances.—The post-resurrection appearances of Jesus are most meaningful. A brief survey of these appearances is in order. The first five were on the day of his resurrection. The sixth was on the first day of the week (Sunday) one week later. The remaining appearances cannot be definitely placed on Sunday, although some interpreters have suggested this as an interesting possibility.

Jesus appeared to Mary Magdalene in the garden where he had been buried. The story is beautifully told in John 20:11–18. When Mary knew the identity of the One who had spoken to her, she was so joyful that she laid hold of him as though she would never let him go. Jesus rebuked her gently. In paraphrase he said, "You must not cling to me as though you would never let me go away again. I was dead; now I am alive and with you again. However, I am not to stay here; I am to ascend to the Father."

The familiar English translation of Jesus' words, "Touch me not," is unfortunate and has led to erroneous deductions. The Greek construction is the negative μή plus the present imperative. As such it prohibits the continuance of an action already in progress. What Jesus really said was, "Stop holding me." An accurate translation is seen in several modern translations. Compare the following: Revised Standard Version, "Do not hold me"; Goodspeed, "You must not cling to me"; Weymouth, "Do not cling to me"; Williams, "Stop clinging to me so." The force of the construction is recognized by the lexicographers.[10]

Shortly after he appeared to Mary, Jesus appeared to the group of women who had gone to the tomb to complete the anointing of his body. This account (Matt. 28:9-10) indicates that the women fell to clasp his feet in adoration and worship. He did not rebuke them as he had Mary; their attitude was entirely different. He sent a message by them to the disciples.

Late in the afternoon of the day of his resurrection he appeared to two disciples on the road to Emmaus (Luke 24: 13-32). This is one of the jewels of Luke's beautiful Gospel. Two disciples—Cleopas and an unnamed person (perhaps Cleopas' wife)—sad and discouraged, walked the dusty road from Jerusalem to their home. As they talked of the things related to the death of their Master, Jesus joined them. There seems to have been nothing spectacular about his joining them. Perhaps Jesus came in from a side road or arose from a place

[10] Thayer, op. cit., p. 70.

38

where he was seated beside the road. As he walked with Cleopas and his companion, Jesus listened for a while and then inquired about the subject of their conversation. Cleopas said, "You must be the only person in Jerusalem who does not know about these things!"

Then Cleopas went on to explain about Jesus, the mighty Prophet whom they "had hoped" was to redeem Israel. But now he had been put to death. There were strange stories told by some women who had gone to the tomb; they had returned to declare that the tomb was empty and that angels had announced that Jesus had been raised from the dead. Unable to believe the women, some of the men went to the tomb. They found it empty, but they saw no angels and no risen Jesus. Hope died.

Then Jesus began to speak. He traced through the Old Testament the indications that the purpose of God included the suffering and death but also the certain triumph of his Son. The hearts of the two were strangely moved as they listened. They remembered the glorious nights they had spent in the presence of Jesus; they remembered the emptiness of the nights since his death. It was nearly night again. How wonderful it would be to have One whose words made their hearts burn with the old fire to pass this night in their home.

Upon the disciples' invitation their Companion of the road went into their home. At mealtime he broke and blessed the bread in the old familiar custom. Eyes which had been blind to his identity (v. 16) were opened to the realization that this was the living Christ (v. 31). With news too good to keep even for one night, they returned to Jerusalem to report to the disciples that Jesus was really alive. In Jerusalem they heard of a fourth appearance of Jesus on that day. This appearance was to Simon Peter alone (Luke 24:34; 1 Cor. 15:5). No record is given of what transpired at that appearance.

On that same evening Jesus appeared to the disciples in the

upper room (Mark 16:14; Luke 24:36–43; John 20:19–25). Thomas was absent, but the remaining ten were present with the doors firmly closed because they feared they might suffer the same fate which their Leader had met. Suddenly they were aware of the presence of Jesus with them in the room. It was more than a spiritual presence. When they thought in their terror that they were seeing a ghost, Jesus demonstrated the reality of his bodily presence: he spoke; he showed them nail-scarred hands and feet; he invited them to touch his body; he ate in their presence. Here is the mystery of his body —a thing beyond human comprehension and explanation. His was a real body, but it was not subject to the ordinary limitations of time, space, and material as it had been before his crucifixion.

One week from that day Jesus appeared to the disciples again (John 20:26–31). This time Thomas was present. He had refused to believe the report of the disciples that Jesus had appeared to them. "You say that he invited you to handle his body? Very well, when I can feel the nail scars in his hands and the sword wound in his side, I will believe, too." At this time he received that invitation from Jesus. "Put your finger here and see my hands; and put out your hand and put it on my side; do not be unbelieving, be believing." The record does not indicate that Thomas needed to do so. Evidently the sight of Jesus convinced him as it had the others; his response was a reverent, "My Lord, and my God."

The seventh appearance of Jesus was to a group of seven disciples by the Sea of Galilee (John 21:1–23). Heavyhearted and empty-handed, they were coming to shore in the boat. On the beach stood a man who called across the water, "Have you caught anything?" Every man who has fished all night and caught nothing can understand the short, heavy reply, "No." The Stranger suggested that they try a spot on the right side of the boat. With fisherman's alacrity to try any suggestion, they cast the nets and found them filled with fish. That was sufficient proof for John. Turning to his companion, he said, "Peter, that is the Lord." Impulsive Simon could not wait to bring fish and boat to shore. He jumped overboard to swim to shore and confronted a striking sight. There was Jesus, with bread and fish cooked and ready for breakfast! From an object lesson as well as from a question and answer period Peter learned many things that day: Jesus could provide for his needs; Jesus had work for him to do; his first concern must be to do that work.

Jesus appeared to a group of more than five hundred people on a mountain in Galilee (Matt. 28:16–20; Mark 16:15–18; 1 Cor. 15:6). They saw him and worshiped him. Even while some doubted the reality of his appearance, he spoke, giving them the commission to go with his authority and make disciples, to baptize these disciples, and to teach them the Christian way of life. He assured them that they would not go alone; he would be with them.

Paul recorded (1 Cor. 15:7) that Jesus appeared to James. No other record of this appearance is given. Early Christian belief was that this James was the half-brother of Jesus and that by this appearance James was converted to the view that Jesus was really the Christ.

Perhaps Paul's reference (1 Cor. 15:7) to Jesus' appearance to all the apostles may be the same as Luke's account (Acts 1:3–8) of the last appearance. There is uncertainty as to the correct chronology. At this time the disciples persisted in asking, "Are you going to restore Israel to her proper political position now?" Jesus' answer indicated knowledge withheld, power promised, and a task assigned.

After assigning to the disciples the task of bearing personal witness for him from Jerusalem to the uttermost part of the earth, Jesus was strangely lifted up from the earth. A cloud came under him. When the cloud disappeared, he, too, had disappeared. Messengers of God appeared to assure the disciples that Jesus would return some day in the same manner in which he had gone away—visibly, mysteriously, personally, and victoriously. What more fitting close could be desired for such a life? He came from heaven. He became a man born of the virgin Mary through the power of the Holy Spirit. He lived a sinless life. He died a vicarious death. He experienced a glorious resurrection. He returned to his home in heaven.

In other New Testament books.—The resurrection of Jesus has a place in other New Testament books. From the foregoing review of the resurrection accounts in the Four Gospels it is clear that this event was a most important part of Christian thought and preaching in the period of spoken gospel tradition as well as during the period of the formation of written documents. Apostolic thought and preaching as presented in Acts and the Epistles made much of the resurrection of Jesus and its significance.

The importance of the fact of Jesus' resurrection is found in the opening pages of the book of Acts. The account in Acts fits into the closing account in the Gospel of Luke in such a way that the Luke-Acts writing may be presented as a whole. Luke tells (Acts 1:3) that during a period of forty days following his resurrection Jesus appeared to his disciples and proved to them by many unmistakable ways that he had actually been raised from the dead. The burden of his teaching during these appearances was the future of the disciples as witnesses for Christ.

Other passages in Acts emphasize the fact of Jesus' resurrection. In Acts 1:23–26 the successor to Judas was chosen to fill out the apostolic twelve. One of the requirements was that the one chosen had to be a witness to the resurrection of Jesus. Again, in Acts 2:27–32, in his sermon at Pentecost Peter used Psalm 16:10–11 to voice confidence that God did not permit death and decay to hold his holy One (Jesus); he loosed him

42

from the clutches of death and exalted him to lordship. The apostles were all witnesses of this (v. 32). In the days that followed, the apostles gave powerful and convincing witness to the resurrection of Jesus (Acts 4:33).

Three sections of Acts record the post-resurrection appearance of Jesus to Saul of Tarsus, who was to become Paul the apostle (Acts 9:1–22; 22:3–16; 26:1–20). The first account is a part of Luke's narrative concerning the work of persecution conducted by Saul and its termination with Saul's Damascus road experience. In the other two passages Paul relates in his own way the dramatic experience; once he told it in defending himself before the Jews in Jerusalem; on the other occasion he told it in his appearance before Festus and Agrippa. With authority from the Sanhedrin, Saul was journeying toward Damascus for the purpose of arresting refugee Christians and returning them to Jerusalem for trial. Many factors in his experience must have paved the way for the momentous event which occurred. At midday there came upon Saul a light brighter than the noontime sun on the white sands of Syria. A voice arrested him in words of rebuke for his work of persecution. Out of this experience Saul came to ask, "What must I do?"

The question related to a completely new direction in Saul's life. As a Pharisee and a zealous rabbi, Saul had had but one purpose in life—to do what God wanted done. Now he knew that what he had been doing was not what God wanted done. His question virtually means, "If what I have been doing is not right, show me what is right and I will do it." In the experiences which followed he was told what to do, and he set himself to the task as one who did not look back.

What was it that convinced him that he had been wrong? It was the appearance to him of the same risen Christ who had appeared to others. A Pharisee who believed in the life of the spirit beyond the death of the body, Saul would not have been

43

convinced by a "ghost" manifestation. In 1 Corinthians 15:8 Paul placed this appearance in the same category with the other post-resurrection appearances. By this manifestation Saul was convinced that the Christians had been right in their report that Jesus had been raised from the dead. It was this conviction which turned him from his role of persecution to his role of preaching in the synagogues of Damascus that Jesus was the Son of God (Acts 9:20).

Paul voiced this conviction often in his writings as well as in his preaching. In Romans 1:4 he stated that from the viewpoint of the flesh Jesus was of the seed of David but that his powerful resurrection declared him to be the Son of God. In Romans 4:24 Paul related the resurrection of Jesus to justification, and in Romans 6:7–10 he indicated that Jesus died but that he was raised to be forever free from death. By faith the believer is dead to his previous relationship to sin and the law and is joined to the risen Christ.

Paul realized that there were those who would stumble at belief in the resurrection of Jesus. This problem is reflected particularly in Romans 10:6–7 and Ephesians 4:9. In Romans 10:6–7 Paul stated that one who is made righteous by faith stumbles neither at the doctrine of the incarnation (asking who shall ascend to heaven to bring Christ down) nor the resurrection (asking who shall descend into the grave to bring Christ up from the dead). The righteousness which is by faith accepts the total redemptive work of God in Christ.

The Ephesians 4:9 passage treats a similar problem but points up incarnation and ascension rather than incarnation and resurrection. The theme discussed is Christ's giving of spiritual gifts for the equipping of his ministers for their service. Paul made rather free use of Psalm 68:18 to teach that when Christ ascended he gave gifts for the use of his ministers in carrying on his work. Then he turned aside from that point to explain that the ascension of Christ implied a previous descent. The same Christ who descended in the incarnation experience ascended to heaven when his redemptive purpose was completed. Doubtless "resurrection" is embraced in the total "ascension," in Paul's thinking.

In other places Paul simply affirmed his faith in the resurrection of Jesus without elaboration (Rom. 14:9; 1 Cor. 15:4–8; Phil. 3:10–11; 2 Tim. 2:8). In still others he stressed the agent of the resurrection. God raised Jesus (Rom. 8:11; Gal. 1:1; Eph. 1:20; Col. 2:12; 1 Thess. 1:10); Jesus was raised through the glory of the Father (Rom. 6:4). In this view that the resurrection of Jesus was through the power of God Paul was in agreement with his fellow Christians and ministers. This is observed in the witness of the disciples in the days following Pentecost (Acts 3:15; 5:30; 26:4–10). It was a continuing witness in preaching (Acts 10:40) and writing (Heb. 13:20; 1 Peter 1:20).

The nature of Jesus' body.—What was the nature of Jesus' body after the resurrection? Can what took place in the transformation be known? Here is an area where dogmatism is to be deplored. The entire phenomenon must be approached with reverent caution. W. T. Conner, having reviewed New Testament evidence for the resurrection of Jesus, stated emphatically: ". . . on the basis of the evidence given in the New Testament I maintain that the resurrection of Jesus included the raising of his body from the dead." [11] But he showed a reverent caution in discussing the nature of Jesus' body, as do other writers.[12]

There is much mystery about the nature of Jesus' body after the resurrection. It was a tangible body: the disciples

---

[11] W. T. Conner, *The Resurrection of Jesus* (Nashville: Sunday School Board of the Southern Baptist Convention, 1926), p. 43.

[12] Hayes, *op. cit.;* James Orr, *The Resurrection of Jesus* (London: Hodder and Stoughton, n.d.); Milligan, *op. cit.;* G. H. Trench, *The Crucifixion and Resurrection of Christ* (London: John Murray, 1908).

saw Jesus (Mark 16:14; John 20:18; 1 Cor. 9:1, etc.), and he talked with them (Matt. 28:18–20; Luke 24:17, 25 ff., etc.). The women who met him on the path clasped his feet (Matt. 28:9), and apparently Mary Magdalene, too, clung to him. He invited Thomas to handle his body (John 20:27). There is no evidence that Thomas did so, but it is most unlikely that Jesus would have invited him to if it had not been possible. He ate in the presence of the disciples (Luke 24:42–43). All this indicates that his was a real body; he was no ghost.

It was a transcendent body. All the above is not to be understood as meaning that Jesus' resurrection was merely the restoration of his body to the nature and functions which it had known before his death. This was no mere resuscitation such as had been experienced by Lazarus, the daughter of Jairus, or the son of the widow at Nain. It was not restoration to the natural plane of life. Jesus' body was not subject to time, space, or material objects. The Master appeared in a room where the doors and windows were closed (John 20:19–26). He vanished from the sight of two who broke bread with him at Emmaus, leaving them amazed but supremely happy (Luke 24:31). He had walked with them to Emmaus, but when they returned to Jerusalem to report the fact, they learned of another appearance that same day in Jerusalem (Luke 24:33–34).

Apparently his body was so transformed and glorified that it had powers which transcended the ordinary operation of laws in the realm of the material and natural level of life. Once it had known the limitations of suffering and death. After the resurrection this was no longer true. Tangible—transcendent! In that seeming paradox the phenomenon must be left. As his precrucifixion body had been adapted to the needs of life in this world, so his resurrection body was adapted to the needs of the new plane of life. The reality of it is too sublime to be grasped by finite minds. There the writers of the New Testament left it; there must we leave it.

The Resurrection of Others

An investigation of the doctrine of the resurrection in the New Testament must take into consideration not only the religious thought of the first century but the religious ideas of the Hebrew people in the centuries before.

Hebrew Beliefs

In previous discussion we have observed that the Old Testament concept of future survival was, at the best, very dim. There is much of uncertainty which pervades the entire atmosphere of the concept. Charles, who is one of the outstanding scholars on Hebrew life and thought, finds in the Old Testament two concepts of the nature of man.[13]

One Old Testament view of man sees him as made up of three parts—body, spirit, and soul. The body is the physical part of man. The spirit is the breath of God which animates the body. The soul is the functioning of the animated body. According to this view, when death comes the soul is extinguished. As the body returns to the earth, the spirit or breath returns to God. Charles holds that this view was historically the parent of later Sadduceeism, which taught that there was neither spirit to survive the death of the body nor resurrection of the body (Acts 23:8).

Charles finds another view of man in the Old Testament which represents man as a creature of two parts—the physical body and the soul, or spirit, which were almost identical. The spirit was looked upon as the soul in its stronger emotional expression. This intensity was taken from the individual at death, and the soul alone went to the life beyond or to Sheol. In both of these views one thing is apparent: something in the nature of man survives the death of the body.

[13] R. H. Charles, *Religious Development Between the Old and the New Testaments* (New York: Henry Holt & Co., Inc., n.d.), pp. 124-33.

47

This idea finds variety of expression. Genesis 35:18 states that when Rachel died her soul departed from her. The word used for the soul here is *nephesh*. Ecclesiastes 12:7 says that when death comes, the body returns to the earth from which it came, and the spirit returns to God who gave it. The word here for spirit is *ruach*. The meaning of this verse is disputed. Interpreters are divided on whether or not the *ruach* continues to live as a separate entity with God.

It is clear that in Hebrew thought something survived in some way the death of the body. An illustration of this is an ancient Hebrew tradition that when the body died the soul, having gone out, lingered near for three days but departed at the first indication of decomposition.[14] This tradition is interesting in the light of Martha's statement to Jesus regarding Lazarus' having been dead *four* days (John 11:39).

Reference is frequently made to the "shade" concept in the Old Testament. This idea is represented in 1 Samuel 28:7–20. The occasion is the visit of Saul to the woman of Endor to request that she bring Samuel from the region of the dead in order that he might advise Saul about his future activities. Whatever interpretation one gives to what happened in the experience of Saul and the woman, it is clear that the passage reflects the concept of some sort of survival after death. The woman was frightened at what she saw and cried out that she saw gods ascending out of the earth (v. 13). The word that is translated "gods" is the Hebrew word *elohim*. This word is used variously in the Old Testament. Sometimes it means God. Other times it means judges or kings, great ones of the earth. Still other times it means shades of the departed.

The life which survived the death of the body was a rather

---

[14] Hermann L. Strack und Paul Billerbeck, "Das Evangelium nach Markus, Lukas und Johannes und die Apostelgeschichte," *Kommentar zum Neuen Testament aus Talmud und Midrash* (Munich: C. H. Becksche Verlagsbuchhandlung, 1924), II, 544; Adolf Schlatter, *Das Evangelist Johannes* (Stuttgart: Calwer Vereinsbuchhandlung, 1930), pp. 250–51.

shadowy existence. Sheol was a land of forgetfulness (Psalm 88:12) and a land of silence (Psalm 94:17; 115:17). Those in that land possessed some degree of self-consciousness and some power of movement and speech (Isa. 14:9–20). In some instances, at any rate, they were thought of as possessing some knowledge of future events and were called upon to give information to the living (1 Sam. 28:13–20). Racial identity was preserved and those who had been slain in battle bore indications of violent death (Ezek. 32:17–32).

Unquestionably the idea of survival after death is reflected in Job 13:14–15 and 19:25–27. This last passage is one of the highest expressions of the venture of faith as it reaches out toward the idea of a future life. In Psalms 16, 17, 49, and 73 there are indications of hope for a blessed life beyond death. Psalms 49 and 73 express belief that the highest blessedness of the righteous is uninterrupted communion with God.

What was the Old Testament concept of resurrection? Here again there are only a limited number of references and in some cases uncertainty of interpretation. The resurrection of the individual is at times seen only as a corporate part of the resurrection of the nation of Israel (Isa. 26:19) to share in the messianic kingdom.[15] It appears, too, that at first the resurrection was the sole privilege of the righteous. According to Isaiah 24–27 there is no resurrection for the wicked. The resurrection of the righteous will be a joyous experience because of the fellowship with God.

Knudson [16] holds that the Hebrew concept of future survival developed along definite lines. First, as the Hebrew became conscious of the importance of the individual over against the importance of the nation, his thinking turned to the idea of the ultimate destiny of the individual. Second, in Job, at least,

---

[15] Charles, *op. cit.*, pp. 113, 120.
[16] Albert C. Knudson, *The Religious Teaching of the Old Testament* (New York: Abingdon-Cokesbury Press, 1918), pp. 394–95.

the idea of God's retribution is carried over into the experience of man beyond death. Third, the bliss of fellowship with God on an individual and personal basis came to be looked upon as the highest expression of good and to be related to the idea of the survival after death.

An investigation of the doctrine of the resurrection in Christian thinking must take into consideration, too, the place of the doctrine in the thinking of Hebrew writers during the intertestamental period. As the Old Testament closed, the doctrine of future survival was more clearly stated than earlier and was beginning to take definite shape. Intertestamental literature reveals much progress in the direction of the concept of future survival to be found later in the New Testament. The movement was away from the idea of the resuscitation of the body and its restoration to prior human functions and toward the idea of individual survival and individual blessedness in heaven or misery in Gehenna.

The writings of the two centuries preceding the time of Christ and the first century of the Christian era reflect definite belief in survival after death and in the doctrine of the resurrection. This view is found in the books which seem to have been most read and appreciated by the Jewish people and by the early Christians, i.e., 1 Enoch, the Testament of the Twelve Patriarchs, 2 Enoch, 2 Baruch, and 4 Ezra. The development was moving rapidly in the direction of what will be found in full expression in the New Testament.

The New Testament Era

When the Hebrew writers and thinkers reached the period which is covered by the New Testament, the lines of thinking on the subject of the resurrection were rather definitely drawn. There were two major religious parties among the Hebrew people in the first century—the Pharisees and the Sadducees. Perhaps there is no point at which the difference between the two is more keenly marked than on the view of future survival. These differences are reflected in several instances in the New Testament.

One of these instances was the occasion of Jesus' controversy with the Sadducees over the doctrine of the resurrection (Matt. 22:23–33). In verse 23 Matthew states that the entire point of the discussion was the fact that the Sadducees denied the resurrection of the dead. Their story was the kind of story that would greatly confuse the Pharisees because of their views of the resurrection. If the former relationships and functions of life were to be maintained in the resurrection, then the question of the Sadducees was a very confusing question. The Pharisees believed that such was the nature of the resurrection, and doubtless the Sadducees had used this story to confuse them many times.

This difference of opinion at the point of this doctrine is reflected, too, in Paul's trial before the Sanhedrin (Acts 23: 6–10). When Paul observed that the Sanhedrin was made up of both Sadducees and Pharisees, he explained to them that he was being tried for proclaiming one of the doctrines precious to the Pharisees—the doctrine of the resurrection. The Pharisees and the Sadducees split in dissension. Luke explains in verse 8 that they did so because while the Sadducees deny both the life of the spirit beyond the death of the body and the resurrection, the Pharisees hold to both doctrines.

Every student of the life of Paul has been amused at Paul's strategy on this occasion. The Pharisees stated that they could find no fault in Paul and that if he had received some word of revelation, they did not want to oppose him lest they be fighting against God. The Sadducees were not willing to accept this, and it seemed that Paul would be torn limb from limb between the two parties. He was rescued from this position by the soldiers, and his subsequent trials were before civil courts. There can be no question that among the Hebrew people the doctrine of the resurrection was one of very lively discussion.

Greek thinking in New Testament times gave still another approach. The Greeks held to the immortality of the soul but rejected the resurrection of the body. To them material was evil and only spirit was good. The height of blessedness for the spirit would be to cast off the limitations of the body.

The Greek denial of the resurrection was reflected in Paul's experience in Athens. When Paul preached Jesus and his resurrection, the Athenians mocked him, making fun not only of his Greek speech but of the doctrine which he was preaching (Acts 17:18).

Interpretation is divided on why the philosophers mocked Paul. The Greek word for Jesus is a masculine noun, and the Greek word for resurrection is a feminine noun. In the Greek religions every god had a corresponding goddess. It appears that the men of Athens were saying that Paul was preaching a new pair of gods—Jesus and "Resurrection." That much is clear. What is not clear is whether they actually misunderstood Paul's preaching and thought he was presenting two new gods or whether they were using that way to scoff at his teaching of the resurrection.

These Greeks took Paul to Mars' Hill for further discussion and listened attentively as he spoke to them concerning the unknown God who has created man and who makes demands as to what man is to be. But when Paul spoke again of the resurrection of Jesus, they started mocking again; while some rejected him outright, others, dismissing him for the present, indicated that they would hear more of his views in the future. The entire passage shows that the Greeks were acquainted with the concept of resurrection although they did not accept it.

There are some passages in the New Testament which are basic to the Christian view of the resurrection. It seems wise to give an interpretation of these passages and let that interpretation direct the further discussion of the subject. No view of the resurrection can be accepted which will not stand the test of the exposition of these basic passages of Scripture. Every view of the resurrection must explain these passages in ways consistent with the principles of exegesis of the Scriptures. In their entirety the passages will touch on many important teachings. For the purpose at hand, however, attention must be restricted to the teaching of the passage as it relates to the subject of the resurrection.

Interpretation [17] of John 5:24-29

This passage is, in many ways, one of the most dramatic in all the Gospel of John. It is representative of a technique found particularly in the Fourth Gospel—that of using a word or an idea in two ways for the purpose of contrast. Even a casual reading of the Fourth Gospel will show the technique of Jesus in using such a play on words. He will discuss material bread and over against that, the bread that comes down from heaven; or in similar fashion, he will discuss the word "water" or "birth" or "spirit" or "light," moving from one use of the term to another in dramatic fashion. In this passage he uses this technique in discussing two kinds of quickening—the spiritual quickening of regeneration (vv. 24-27) and the spiritual quickening of resurrection (vv. 28-29).

The major emphasis in this passage is on two works which

[17] A. Plummer, *The Gospel According to St. John* ("Cambridge Greek Testament for Schools and Colleges Series" [Cambridge: Cambridge University Press, 1896]); Marcus Dods, "The Gospel of St. John," *The Expositor's Greek Testament* (Grand Rapids: Wm. B. Eerdmans Publishing Co., n.d.); Alvah Hovey, "Commentary on the Gospel of John," *An American Commentary on the New Testament* (Philadelphia: American Baptist Publication Society, 1885); William Hendriksen, "Exposition of the Gospel According to John," *New Testament Commentary* (Grand Rapids: Baker Book House, 1953); R. C. H. Lenski, *The Interpretation of St. John's Gospel* (Columbus: Lutheran Book Concern, 1942); Wilbert F. Howard, "The Gospel According to St. John," *The Interpreter's Bible* (Nashville: Abingdon Press, 1952).

the Father has assigned to the Son. One is quickening the dead, and the other is pronouncing judgment. In verses 24–25 Jesus explained that the Son performs the work of spiritually quickening the dead, i.e., regeneration, and pronouncing judgment upon those who refuse to hear the Son of God. This is a work which he performs in the present. When he said, "The hour comes and now is," he was saying to the Jewish listeners that the Messianic Age had already broken into history in his presence among them. Jesus said that he had power from the Father to work the spiritual miracle of life in those who will hear him. This was a rather startling thing for Jesus to say to his hearers, and they wondered at it.

In verse 28 Jesus told them to stop their marveling. He told them of another quickening of the dead and of a judgment which would be carried out as a part of his work. This quickening of the dead and carrying out of judgment was for the future and it related to the doctrine of the resurrection which was well known to the Jews. Jesus said that the hour comes (he cannot say "and now is," as he did in verse 25) when all who are in the tombs will hear his voice and will come forth, those who have done good to a "life" kind of resurrection and those who have done evil to a "judgment" kind of resurrection. But both are to be raised. If Jesus' hearers marveled at his claim to quicken the spirits of men in regeneration, they would marvel all the more at his claim to quicken the bodies of men in the resurrection.

Several terms deserve specific treatment. The expression "the dead" (v. 25) is a metaphorical reference to the spiritual dead who come to spiritual life through the process of regeneration. In contrast, the expression "in the tombs" (v. 28) refers to the bodies of those who have been taken in physical death who are to be quickened through the experience of resurrection from the dead. Again, in verse 28 the word "all" is important. This emphasis is in line with other references in the

New Testament which present the resurrection of all men, both righteous and unrighteous. The idea is positively affirmed in Acts 24:15 and implied in such passages as Matthew 7:21–23; 13:36–43; 16:24–27; and Revelation 20:12–13.

This statement from Jesus is one of the foundation statements for the view of one general resurrection at the last day. The best of the expositors affirm this interpretation and hold that there is no basis whatever for the idea of two separate resurrections at two different periods of time. The contrast here is not between two different times when men are to be raised but between the different kinds of men who are to be raised, those who have practiced good and those who have practiced evil. Those who have practiced good (and this must be understood in relationship to Jesus' statement in verse 24 about hearing his word and believing on the One who sent him) will be raised to a resurrection which is described by the term "life." On the other hand, those who have practiced worthless things (and they must be understood as those who do not believe in the One that sent Christ) shall be raised to a resurrection which is described by the word "judgment," and which can mean only condemnation.

The many commentaries which have been consulted are unanimous in agreeing that Jesus' teaching here can refer to nothing short of the resurrection of the body. Nothing is said in this passage about the time of the resurrection other than that "the hour comes." In John 6, however, Jesus specifically stated that the resurrection will be "at the last day" (vv. 39–40, 44, and 54).

Interpretation [18] of 1 Thessalonians 4:13–18

This is probably the first of Paul's epistles to the churches. The spirit of hope and encouragement which pervades the

[18] Commentaries especially helpful on this passage are: John W. Bailey, "The First and Second Epistles to the Thessalonians," *The Interpreter's Bible* (Nash-

epistle is nowhere more clearly seen than in this paragraph. All of the background of the paragraph is not known. It appears from both Thessalonian letters that Paul had preached much on the theme of the Lord's return during his ministry in Thessalonica. It appears, too, that in the months since he had left the church there had come to be great concern on the part of many Thessalonian Christians about the relationship of the Christian dead to the return of the Lord. It may be that news of this difficulty was brought to Paul by Timothy. Of course, it is entirely possible that a letter to Paul requested help. Whatever the source of his information, Paul moved to dispel from the minds of the Thessalonian Christians any difficulty over this problem.

Paul began the discussion with a statement that he did not wish the Thessalonians to be uninformed concerning "them that fall asleep" (v. 13), indicating that his discussion would relate to those who had died and to the concern of the Thessalonian Christians about them. Paul did not tell the Thessalonians that they were not to grieve for lost loved ones. Grief is normal for one who has lost a loved one in death; in many cases it has proved to have genuine value. Paul did say, however, that when Christian loved ones were lost in death, sorrow for them was not to be hopeless because an element of hope has been introduced into human experience. The fact that there was One who had already been raised from the

---

ville: Abingdon Press, 1955); John Calvin, *Commentary on the Epistles of Paul the Apostle to the Philippians, Colossians, and Thessalonians* (Grand Rapids: Wm. B. Eerdmans Publishing Co., 1948); B. H. Carroll, "James, I and II Thessalonians and I and II Corinthians," *An Interpretation of the English Bible* (New York: Fleming H. Revell Co., 1916); James Denny, "The Epistles to the Thessalonians," *The Expositor's Bible* (New York: Eaton and Mains, n.d.); James Moffat, "The First and Second Epistles to the Thessalonians," *The Expositor's Greek Testament* (Grand Rapids: Wm. B. Eerdmans Publishing Co., n.d.); William Hendriksen, "Exposition of I and II Thessalonians," *New Testament Commentary* (Grand Rapids: Baker Book House, 1955); R. C. H. Lenski, *The Interpretation of St. Paul's Epistles to the Colossians, to the Thessalonians, to Timothy, to Titus and to Philemon* (Columbus: Wartburg Press, 1946).

dead was an indication that the barriers of death had been broken, that ultimately death itself will be totally destroyed.

This element of hope in the resurrection is based on faith in the resurrection of Jesus (v. 14). The verse reads, "For if we believe that Jesus died and rose again, even so them who are fallen asleep in Jesus will God bring with him." The sentence is what is known in Greek grammar as a first-class conditional sentence. In this construction the reality of the action of the verb is affirmed. The word "if" raises no question about belief in the resurrection of Jesus; rather, it affirms belief in the resurrection of Jesus. The word could very accurately be translated "since." It is apparent that Paul was saying that belief in the resurrection of the dead is based on belief that Jesus rose from the dead. Specifically the ones with whom he was dealing in this passage are those Christians who had died. When the Lord returns to the earth, he will be accompanied by those who have gone in death and whose spirits have enjoyed the blessed presence and fellowship of the Lord since death came to the body.

In verse 15 Paul indicates the source of his information; his teaching was based on a revelation of the Lord. He did not tell the exact time and mode of the revelation. It could be that he based his teaching on some words of Christ which were not recorded in the gospels. The gospel writers said that Jesus did and said many things other than those which they recorded. On the other hand, it could be that Paul received this knowledge by special revelation. The New Testament records experiences of Paul in which a divine visitation was made to him in some emergency situation. It could be that to such an experience as that he owed this teaching. Whatever it is, he affirmed that it came from the Lord.

The teaching is that which follows. Those who are living at the time of the Lord's return will have no advantage over those who have died. Paul used the first personal pronoun "we" in referring to the ones living when the Lord returns. This is variously interpreted. Some hold that it is purely a rhetorical or editorial reference and as such says nothing of Paul's hope or expectation of being in the number of those living when the Lord returns. Still others hold that it is a reference to Paul, Silas, and Timothy who are mentioned together in the salutation of the epistle (1:1). For the most part, however, the word "we" is interpreted as an indication that Paul shared the hope of the early Christians of being alive when the Lord returned. It would do no violence to the principle of the inspiration of the Scriptures if Paul should not be alive when the Lord returns. The time of the Lord's return was the thing that was concealed even from those who wrote about it.

The more important part of this verse is the statement "will have no advantage over those who have fallen asleep." It is recognized that the King James Version translation "prevent" does not express in twentieth-century English what Paul had in mind. The American Standard Version translation "precede" also leaves something lacking by way of clear expression.

As the Thessalonian Christians looked to the glorious experience of the Lord's return, they were troubled that their loved ones had died before that experience would miss some of the glory of it. Paul's assurance was that such was not the case. He used a Greek construction of the double negative which, while thought of in English as bad grammar, was in Greek one of the strongest possible ways of making a positive statement. Literally translated, it would be "will not never have an advantage over." It was Paul's way of saying that when the Lord returns the living Christians will have no advantage whatever, no privilege whatever, beyond that of the Christians who will have fallen asleep before his return.

In verse 16 Paul began his explanation of the nature of the Lord's return and its results as far as the Christians are concerned. The Lord himself will descend from heaven. This speaks of the personal appearance of Christ in fulfilment of his promise to return. His coming will be accompanied by startling demonstrations—"with a shout, with a voice of the archangel, and with the trumpet of God." It is not important that the significance of each of these statements be determined. The word "shout" is a word which means a command, usually a military command. The "trumpet of God" has reference to the triumphant note by which God would speak. The identity of the archangel is not important.

This passage should be read in connection with 1 Corinthians 15 to understand Paul's view that the Lord was to return personally to the earth and that his return would mean the resurrection of the dead. Paul was not giving here a detailed program of activity in relationship to the Lord's return. For that reason he said nothing whatever about the resurrection of the unbeliever, nothing about judgment. He was writing for the purpose of comforting troubled minds at one point. The view of Paul on these other matters related to the Lord's return must be found in other parts of his writings, not in this passage.

In this passage Paul did speak of two events as they were related to the Lord's return and as they were related to the problem immediately before him. Two groups of people were awaiting the Lord's return to the earth. One group was made up of the Christians who died before his return and the other group, of the Christians who will be still alive when he returns. Paul spoke of what will happen to them and the order in which it will happen. That is all that he gave in this passage. There is an element of sequence expressed in the two words "first" and "then." Inversion of the words in the first clause will make the meaning clearer: "first the dead in Christ shall rise; then we who are alive who are left will be gathered with them, will be caught up in the clouds to welcome the Lord in the air, and thus we will always be with the Lord." Paul had this in mind when he said that living believers will have no advantage over believers who have died, because when the Lord returns he will first raise the dead and then catch up the living. There will be no longer two groups waiting for the Lord but one group eternally in his presence.

Paul concluded that part of the discussion with his statement, "Comfort one another with these words," that is, "Comfort one another with this truth": nothing, not even death, can make any essential difference in the close relationship existing between the believer and his Lord. Death is to be conquered in resurrection, and when it has been so conquered, there will be no more sleeping in him or waiting for him. There will be only eternity with him.

It has been indicated already that there are other events related to the Lord's return and the resurrection which are not mentioned in this passage. For instance, in 1 Corinthians 15 Paul spoke of the instantaneous transformation of those who are living when the Lord returns. He did not use that terminology here. If it has its parallel in 1 Thessalonians, it would appear to be in that part of verse 15 which speaks of the living believers' being caught up with the Lord and with believers who had already died to make one glorious company for eternity.

Paul believed in God's judgment upon men, but he said nothing of that in this passage. He believed in the eternal destiny of punishment for the unbeliever, but he said nothing of that in this passage. He believed in the resurrection of unbelievers, but he said nothing of that in this passage. Honest exegesis cannot find the idea of two resurrections in this passage. It can find the resurrection of the dead believers and the transformation of the living believers in connection with the Lord's return. Beyond that answers to questions relative to these events must be found in other passages of Scripture.

Interpretation [19] of 1 Corinthians 15

This is one of the most basic New Testament passages on the doctrine of the resurrection of the dead. No treatment of the doctrine can be comprehensive without a careful analysis of this entire passage. Paul's discussion appears to be a part of his answer to a question which had been asked of him by the church at Corinth. In 1 Corinthians 7:1 he made reference to the things concerning which the Corinthians had written to him and took up these matters, beginning in that chapter. This question regarding his view of the resurrection appears to be the final one in the series. Perhaps his view can best be seen by discussing the sections of the chapter.

Basis for the doctrine: 1 Corinthians 15:3–34.—Here belief in the resurrection of others is based on the doctrine of the resurrection of Jesus. This idea is found in many places in the New Testament, among them Acts 4:2, Philippians 3:10–11, 21, 1 Thessalonians 4:14, and 1 Peter 1:3, as well as Jesus' own statement in John 14:19, "Because I live, you also will live."

In 1 Corinthians 15 Paul included the resurrection of Jesus as a basic part of the good news, that is, the gospel, which was being preached in his day. He made four statements with reference to the experience of Jesus in the consummation of his days on the earth: (1) He died. This Paul found to be a

[19] In addition to sources cited through the discussion the following works are most helpful: John Calvin, *op. cit.;* B. H. Carroll, *op. cit.;* Clarence Tucker Craig, "The First Epistle to the Corinthians," *The Interpreter's Bible* (New York: Abingdon-Cokesbury Press, 1953); E. P. Gould, "Commentary on the Epistles to the Corinthians," *An American Commentary on the New Testament* (Philadelphia: The American Baptist Publication Society, 1887); Albert Barnes, *Notes on the New Testament: I Corinthians* (Grand Rapids: Baker Book House, 1949); R. C. H. Lenski, *The Interpretation of St. Paul's First and Second Epistles to the Corinthians* (Columbus: Wartburg Press, 1946); J. J. Lias, *The First Epistle to the Corinthians* ("Cambridge Greek Testament for Schools and Colleges Series" [Cambridge: Cambridge University Press, 1882]).

fulfilment of Old Testament Scriptures. (2) He was buried. (3) He was raised from the dead, and this, too, was in fulfilment of Old Testament Scriptures. (4) He was seen by many people. One of the most significant things in this passage is Paul's use of Greek tenses. There are four verbs that are important. In three of them—died, buried, and appeared—Paul used the aorist tense, which speaks simply of an act that was accomplished.

The other verb, by which Paul referred to the resurrection of Jesus, is in the perfect tense, "He has been raised." The force of the Greek perfect tense is that it describes a state of being which is the result of a completed action. The genius of the tense can be seen in this translation: "Christ is in a state of having been raised from the dead." This is in line with the New Testament teaching that when Christ was raised from the dead his body was so transformed that it could never die again. This idea is basic because it is Paul's view of the resurrection of others as well.

Then, continuing his discussion of the resurrection of Jesus, Paul enumerated six of the post-resurrection appearances of Jesus including the appearance to Paul himself on the road to Damascus. He concluded that part of the discussion by indicating in verse 11 that this gospel of a risen Christ was not one which Paul alone preached. It was the gospel which was being proclaimed by the other preachers of Christ, and it was the gospel which the Corinthians had heard and had believed.

The importance of the resurrection of Jesus in consideration of the general doctrine of the resurrection is set out by Paul in verses 12–34. He began in verse 12 by assuming that Christ had not been raised from the dead. He showed what that would mean to Christian faith and experience. He was arguing from a viewpoint which he could never accept, and in this argument he reduced to the absurd the position which would affirm the resurrection of Christ but deny the resurrection of others. The very fact that Christ has been raised from the dead is a guarantee that the kingdom of death has been invaded, that it has been robbed of a part of its prey, and that this is hope and assurance that ultimately it will be completely destroyed.

Paul's argument is that if there is no such thing as the resurrection from the dead, then Christ has not been raised (v. 13). If Christ has not been raised, several things follow which are of tremendous importance in the Christian religion. If Christ has not been raised, Christian preaching is void of meaning and Christian faith is void of meaning (v. 14). The word which Paul used, sometimes translated "vain," speaks of emptiness. It was a word which described a nutshell from which the kernel had been taken. The *kerygma*, that is, the gospel preached by the early apostles, included the resurrection of Christ as a climactic part. To take that element out of the thing preached and the thing believed would mean emptiness and worthlessness.

More than that, if Christ has not been raised, all who have been preaching his resurrection are false witnesses (v. 15). They have been bearing testimony to the fact that God raised Christ from the dead; if there is no resurrection, God has not raised Christ from the dead, and they have been bearing false testimony. Continuing that suggestion, Paul underscored the truth of it when he said, "If there is no resurrection, then Christ has not been raised" (v. 16). If there is no resurrection from the dead, the empty tomb in Jerusalem will have to be explained in some other way.

This tragedy becomes personal in verses 17–19. If Christ has not been raised, Christian faith is meaningless, and those who have exercised that faith are still under the burden of their sins. They believed that in Christ God had provided the One that he had promised as a Redeemer for sin; but if that which they believed is not true, it is evident that the bur-

63

den of their sins is still upon them and they must look elsewhere for redemption.

Tragic application is made to those who have already died trusting Christ (v. 18). Those who, according to verse 17, have an empty faith and are still in their sins do have time to seek and find a way out of their sins; but this is not true for those who have already died exercising faith in Christ. If Christ has not been raised and if Christian faith is meaningless, those who have died trusting in Christ have perished and there is no opportunity and no salvation for them.

Paul's last statement regarding the tragedy of assuming that there is no resurrection is expressed in verse 19. There he states that if Christians' hope in Christ has been hope where this life only is involved, they are of all men most impoverished. They have missed the main point of faith in Christ if they have limited faith in him to this physical life. Faith in Christ reaches beyond death, which marks the end of physical life, and a man is most impoverished if he does not find in Christ hope for the life beyond.

Having discussed what the assumption that Christ has not been raised would mean to Christian faith, Paul turned in verses 20–34 to affirm the fact of the resurrection of Christ and to relate it to Christian hope. He repeated the perfect tense (which he had used in verse 4) when he said, "But now Christ *has been raised* from the dead." All of Christian witness and faith accepted the proposition that Christ had been raised from the dead, never to die again.

In being thus raised, Christ came to be the first fruits of those who had died. Death was introduced into the world by man. Resurrection also was introduced into the world by man. Through the work of disobedience of one man, Adam, death was introduced in human experience. Through the work of obedience of another man, Christ, resurrection was introduced in human experience. Growing out of man's relationship to Adam there is the experience of death; growing out of relationship to Christ there is the experience of resurrection.

While Paul was in this passage discussing particularly the resurrection of believers, as he did in 1 Thessalonians 4, the statement that in Christ will *all* be made alive in verse 22 seems to be comprehensive. Attention will be given elsewhere specifically to Paul's view of the resurrection of the wicked. Here he indicated that all are to be raised from the dead.

There is, however, a proper sequence in the matter of the resurrection which Paul set out in verse 23. All will be raised, but each in his own order. That order is twofold: Christ was raised first as the *first fruits* of the dead; those who belong to Christ will be raised at his second coming as the *harvest*. The illustration is one familiar to students of the Old Testament. In late spring or early summer the people would go into the wheat fields and gather the first heads of ripened grain. These would be a sacrifice and a promise of the general harvest in due time. As Paul thought of the resurrection of the dead, he saw Christ as the first fruits and others as the general harvest which will be at Christ's second coming.

Whatever happened to Christ in the resurrection and transformation of his body is going to happen to others, the difference being in time. Christ was raised on the third day as the first fruits of resurrection. Others will be raised at his second coming as the general harvest. At that time Christ will deliver the kingdom to the Father as a work that has been completed by his having conquered every enemy including the last enemy—death. When death itself has been conquered so that it can never claim men, Christ's redemptive work will have reached consummation.

The ultimate result of belief or unbelief in the resurrection is indicated in verses 29–34. Belief in the resurrection has, first, an evangelistic incentive. The case of the one who is not a believer but who has a loved one who is a believer might be used as an illustration. That loved one dies. The experience causes the unbeliever to think seriously on the matters of life and death and the beyond. Out of hope of seeing his loved one in the life which is beyond, the unbeliever turns to the Christian faith and to the expression of that Christian faith as it is illustrated in the experience of baptism. This appears to be the meaning of the much-disputed passage of verse 29 regarding the matter of being "baptized for the dead." The preposition translated "for" carries the force of "with reference to" or "because of." [20]

On the other hand, lack of faith in the doctrine of the resurrection leads logically to an emphasis on this life and indulgence of the appetites of the body. This idea of indulgence of the appetites of the flesh was quite commonly accepted. Paul saw it as the logical conclusion to holding that there is no life beyond this physical one. It should be granted that it is certainly doubtful if Paul would say that either of these two extremes would be accepted either by those believing in the resurrection or those denying it. It should be granted, too, that Paul would praise the high ethical advantage of the Christian life for this world even if there were no after life. He was simply showing that, pressed to its ultimate and logical conclusion, faith in the resurrection from the dead is an incentive to man's becoming rightly related to Christ by faith, while denial of the resurrection of the dead, pressed to its ultimate and logical conclusion, puts the emphasis on making the most of this physical life while there is opportunity. Paul even raised the question (v. 32) as to whether or not the sacrifice to win men to God is worthwhile if this life is all.

The power of God: 1 Corinthians 15:35–38.—Paul next

[20] Cf. G. G. Findlay, "St. Paul's Epistle to the Corinthians," *The Expositor's Greek Testament* (Grand Rapids: Wm. B. Eerdmans Publishing Co., n.d.); David Smith, *The Disciple's Commentary on the New Testament* (New York: Ray Long and Richard R. Smith, Inc., 1932), IV, 486.

raised a question (v. 35) which is many times raised today: "How are the dead raised and with what kind of body?" This is not a new question. It was a problem in Jewish religious and Greek philosophical thought. Perhaps some of the concern of the Thessalonian Christians over their dead loved ones stemmed from the fact that the question of the resurrection was a real problem in their minds.

Paul's answer to the question, "How are the dead raised?" is set out in verses 36-38. Very simply—in fact, it might appear as an oversimplification—he answered the question "how" by saying that the resurrection comes through God's power. Since God had the power to give the kind of bodies needed for the physical level of life, he has the power to give the kind of body that will be needed on that eternal and spiritual level of life.

Paul answered by way of illustration, first in the world of *vegetation.* Here is a grain of wheat. It falls into the earth. It experiences the processes of decay that are inherent in its nature, but the wonder-working principle of God brings life out of that death—life on a higher and more transcendent plane, as there comes not one grain of wheat but a beautiful green plant that produces from the one grain many. All this is done through God's power. There is a continuity from the one body to the other, but the second is far more transcendent than the first.

Paul illustrated, too, on the *animal* level. There is one type of body possessed by man; another possessed by four-footed beasts; still another by birds, and another by fish. God has the wisdom and the power to provide the kind of body that each of his creatures needs according to the nature of its life. So he will have the wisdom and the power to provide the kind of bodies that men shall need for the eternal order.

Going beyond this, Paul spoke of the different kinds of *heavenly bodies.* There is one kind of body which is recognized as sun, another as moon, and even the stars are not identical. God has the wisdom and the power to provide these "heavenly" bodies. He also has the wisdom and the power to provide the kind of bodies that will be needed for heavenly habitation. For Paul the answer to the question of "how" was rather simple—it is through God's power. In his controversy with the Sadducees over the problem of resurrection Jesus said that a part of their trouble in their denial of the resurrection was due to the fact that they were not acquainted with the power of God.

The resurrection body: 1 Corinthians 15:39–50.—Verse 42 introduces a transition from the question of how to the question of what kind. Here Paul took up the figure of the grain again. This body will be planted like a seed; it will be raised in resurrection to a higher order of bodily existence. Several contrasts are set out. First, it is planted in corruption and is raised in incorruption. This terminology of corruption and incorruption refers to the "subject-to-decay" nature of this physical body and, in contrast, the "not-subject-to-decay" nature of the body of the resurrection. Second, this body is planted in dishonor and is raised in glory. It is planted a body that has been dishonored because of the defiling presence of sin; it will be raised a glorious body, one that cannot be brought low by sin. Third, it is planted in weakness; it is raised in power. This body has been a limited, handicapped body. It has never been able to measure up to the highest potential of God's plan and purpose. When the body is raised in the resurrection, it will be raised to a condition that will be free of all such limitations and handicaps.

Fourth, it is planted a natural body; it is raised a spiritual body. This is the very heart of all that Paul had to say regarding the nature of the resurrection body. It must be noted, beginning with this statement in verse 44 and going on through verse 49, that Paul's insistence was that the eternal state will be a bodily state, even as the temporal has been a bodily state. He did not say that there is planted a *body* and raised a *spirit*. He said there is planted a *natural body* and raised a *spiritual body*.[21] An adjective is used in each instance to modify the word "body." It is planted a natural ($\psi\upsilon\chi\iota\kappa\acute{o}\nu$) body. It is raised a spiritual ($\pi\nu\epsilon\upsilon\mu\alpha\tau\iota\kappa\acute{o}\nu$) body. Each of the two adjectives has the same type of ending—$\iota\kappa o\nu$. When a Greek adjective ends in this syllable, its meaning is that of adequacy for every need indicated in the word to which it is added. The adjective that is translated "natural" is the Greek word from which the word "physical" is taken.

The earthly body has been *perfectly adapted* to the needs of this *physical plane* of existence; the heavenly body will be a body *perfectly adapted* to the needs of the *spiritual plane* of existence. Paul would insist that it *is* a body. It is at this point that he went beyond both the Jewish concept of resurrection and the Greek concept of the immortality of the soul. Paul saw the resurrection body as a body that is real, but not one restored to its former limited physical nature and function. Likewise, he saw the resurrection body as a bodily state and not merely an eternity of living as a spirit with no body at all.

He related the concept of the body to man's relationship to Adam and to Christ. Out of his relationship to Adam man has a physical body that is subject to decay and to death. Out of his relationship to Christ he is to have a spiritual body that is not subject to decay and to death. As man has experienced a likeness to the first man, Adam, in his physical life, so he will experience a likeness to the second man, Christ, in his spiritual life.

Paul insisted that the spirit will no more exist through eter-

[21] Cf. H. Clavier, "Breves remarques sur la notion de $\sigma\tilde{\omega}\mu\alpha$ $\pi\nu\epsilon\upsilon\mu\alpha\tau\iota\kappa\acute{o}\nu$," *The Background of the New Testament and Its Eschatology*, ed. W. D. Davies and D. Daube (Cambridge: Cambridge University Press, 1956), pp. 342–62.

nity apart from a body than the body has existed through time apart from the spirit. The body has been a physical habitation for the spirit for this physical level of life. The body will also be a spiritual habitation for the spirit for the eternal spiritual life. For Paul there could be no complete personality apart from the resurrection of the body to be the glorious dwelling place for the spirit for eternity. There could be no victory over death unless the body were raised from the dead and so transformed that it could never die again—so transformed that it could be the dwelling place of the spirit for eternity.

Beyond this, Paul said little about the nature of the resurrection body except that which he gave in Philippians 3:20–21. In contrast to the people of this world and the state of their citizenship Paul spoke of believers and their citizenship, which is in heaven. They wait for Jesus Christ, their Lord and Saviour, to come from heaven. When he comes, he will "fashion anew the body of our humiliation, conformed to his glorious body."

In Philippians 2:8 Paul had said that a part of the experience of Jesus in his incarnation was that he humbled himself to accept the human form which was subject to death. Here Paul looked forward to that day when Christ will change human bodies from their state of humiliation and make them to be like his—a glorious body that is not subject to death. What more should Christians want to know about the nature of the bodies that shall be theirs for eternity? They will be like his.

The time of the resurrection: 1 Corinthians 15:50–54.— As Paul took up the question of the time of the resurrection, he introduced the discussion by an emphatic reassertion in verse 50 of all that he had said concerning the nature of a resurrection body. Since decay and change are inherent in the very nature of the earthly body, it is not a fit subject for the spirit's eternal habitation. That which is subject to death cannot dwell eternally where death will be unknown. These earthly bodies will be changed before they become the eternal dwelling places of the spirit.

This change will be realized in one of two ways. Those who have died prior to the Lord's return will be changed in one way, that is, by resurrection; those who are living at the time of the Lord's return will be changed another way, that is, by an instantaneous transformation. This is a mystery, something which calls for revelation. Apart from revelation the experience of man beyond death is clouded in mystery, but Paul revealed the secret of this particular mystery in his discussion. Not all will die, but all will be changed.

This change will take place in connection with the Lord's return. Verse 52 echoes the language of 1 Thessalonians 4:16. In that passage Paul connected the resurrection of the dead with the sounding of the trumpet of God. Here he made the same connection. The blinking of an eyelid is the quickest movement of the human body; that quickly, Paul said, the transformation will take place. The transformation will be experienced both by those who are dead and by those who are living.

In the closing part of verse 52 and through verses 53 and 54, Paul set up a twofold contrast. The dead will be raised incorruptible, i.e., so they will never be subject to death again; the living will be changed so they will never be subject to death. "Corruptible" is used in verse 53 to refer to those who have died, and "mortal" is used to refer to those who are living but subject to death. The corruptible, i.e., those who have died, will be raised incorruptible, i.e., they can never die again. The mortal, i.e., those living but so constituted that they are subject to death, will put on immortality, i.e., they will be changed so they will no longer be subject to death. When these two changes have been made, then will be fulfilled the saying, "Death has been swallowed up in victory."

71

The fact that Paul in this paragraph contrasted living men on the one hand and dead bodies on the other is made more pointed by a historical reference. "Flesh and blood" (v. 50) was frequently used by the Jewish rabbis in reference to natural man as a creature of frailty. The words always applied to living persons. The expression "flesh and blood" refers to the transforming of the living and is set in contrast to the raising of the dead in the term "nor does corruption inherit incorruption." In this section of verses 50–54 Paul made use of *chiasmus,*[22] which is something of a reversed parallelism. Note that in verses 50–51 the living are mentioned first and the dead are mentioned second: flesh and blood (the living)—corruption (the dead); not all sleep (the living)—all to be changed ("all" includes the dead). When Paul enlarged on the discussion in verses 52–54, he reversed that order. He spoke of those who are dead first and those who are living but are subject to death second: corruptible (the dead)—mortal (the living).

Chiasmus

Verse 50	The living = "flesh and blood"	The dead = "corruption"
Verse 51	The living = "not all sleep"	The dead = "all will be changed"—the dead included
Verse 52	The dead = "raised"	The living = "changed"
Verse 53	The dead = "corruptible"	The living = "mortal"
Verse 54	The dead = "corruptible"	The living = "mortal"

There is in the paragraph a very remarkable *negative* assertion followed by a *positive* assertion. The *negative* assertion

[22] From χιασμός, meaning a diagonal arrangement of the separate parts of a proposition.

is that neither those who are living nor those who have died are fit subjects for eternal dwelling with God in their respective states. The *positive* assertion is that both those who are dead as well as those who are living will be changed when the Lord returns. They will be changed into forms which will never again be subject to death. This will indeed mean that death is completely swallowed up in victory.

This view that the expression "flesh and blood" refers to the living rather than to the dead is a very important one. On the basis of understanding it as a reference to the dead, there have been attempts made to show a change in Paul's thinking as shown in three stages in 1 Thessalonians 4, 1 Corinthians 15, and 2 Corinthians 5. That viewpoint represents Paul as thinking in 1 Thessalonians 4 in terms of the resurrection of the body in line with the Jewish view of the restoration of the body to its physical functions. When Paul spoke of the raising of the dead and the catching up of the living, he said nothing about the living's being changed from one form to another, so it is assumed that he had in mind their continuing in their physical forms.

The second step in Paul's thinking would be in 1 Corinthians 15, some time later. He had come to see more of the Greek concept of the immortality of the soul; therefore, he said that bodily existence, that is, flesh and blood, has nothing whatever to do with the eternal state. The third step is an interpretation of 2 Corinthians 5, which holds that when Paul wrote this passage, he had given up the idea of the new body to be given at the time of the Lord's return and held that there would be no resurrection of the body. All an individual receives for eternal dwelling he will receive at the time of his death.

At least two objections to this view may be raised. One is that the view simply will not meet the test of exegesis. The other is that while Paul was never static in his thinking, it is inconceivable that he would have made such radical changes in his thinking in the brief period of time covered by these three epistles. The answer to the problem of the difference between 1 Thessalonians 4 and 1 Corinthians 15 appears to be found in the word "mystery," i.e., a new revelation. Paul was here giving a view which he had not previously given: the transformation of both the living and the dead takes place immediately at the second coming of Christ. Both are transformed to a body which can never be subject to death, and both share in all the glory of the Lord's return.[23]

The result of the resurrection: 1 Corinthians 15:55-58.—The result of this resurrection of the dead at the coming of Christ is that death is completely robbed of its victory over man. Through sin, death has had dominion over man, but through the redemptive work of God through Christ the dominion of both sin and death has been defeated. Victory over sin comes in regeneration; victory over death comes in resurrection. It is Paul's view that God's purpose for man is to redeem him in his total personality. Only through the process of resurrection can this victory be completely realized.

Interpretation of 2 Corinthians 5:1-10

The last in a series of basic passages relating to the doctrine of the resurrection is this controversial section from the writings of Paul. Some interpreters hold that Paul had here given up the idea of the resurrection of the body and was holding to the idea that whatever an individual receives for eternal dwelling he receives at the point of death. Another suggestion

[23] Having presented this total view in class for the last fifteen years, it was most gratifying for the author to find almost the same development in a recent article by the esteemed Professor Jeremias of the University of Göttingen. Joachim Jeremias, "Flesh and Blood Cannot Inherit the Kingdom of God," *New Testament Studies*, II (February, 1956), 151-59. In agreement with the view is Professor Sevenster of Amsterdam. Cf. J. N. Sevenster, "Einige Bemerkungen 'über den "Zwischenzustand" bei Paulus,'" *New Testament Studies*, I (May, 1955), 291-96.

is that man will receive at death an intermediate body which he will give up at the resurrection for the eternal body. Those who hold these views do so in spite of the fact that scholars are practically unanimous in rejecting such interpretations.[24]

The list of authorities who hold that in this passage Paul was presenting the idea of the disembodied state until the second coming of Christ and the resurrection of the body at that time is a most impressive one: Filson, Alford, Gould, Barnes, Reid, Lias, Plummer, Erdman, Denny, Carroll, Massie, Bernhard, Lange, Goudge, Robertson, MacKintosh, Williams, Hodge, Ockenga, and Stanley. It is to be expected that among these interpreters there would be some element of disagreement in detailed interpretation. Such is the case, though they all hold to the idea of a disembodied state between the death of the individual and his resurrection at the second coming of Christ.

The background of this passage and its setting in the epistle is of importance in the matter of interpretation. Beginning with 4:1, Paul discussed his manner of performing his apostolic duties. He had performed his duties in absolute sincerity (vv. 1-6) and in the face of great difficulties (vv. 7-18). He spoke of having this treasure of the responsibility of preaching Christ in earthen vessels, i.e., perishable vessels, human bodies.

Beginning with verse 16, Paul indicated that he did not despair as in the turmoil of his missionary ministries he found his physical body wearing out daily. Though he was losing ground physically, he was gaining ground spiritually. More and more his interest came to be not in things that are seen, the temporal things, but in things that are unseen, the eternal things (v. 18). Review of his physical weariness caused his thinking to turn to his hope for the future, set out in 5:1-10.

This passage begins with an affirmation of faith that even if

[24] Floyd V. Filson, "The Second Epistle to the Corinthians," *The Interpreter's Bible* (New York: Abingdon-Cokesbury Press, 1953).

the earthly tent be completely worn out, the Christian has a building from God that is eternal in the heavens. In other words, the complete wearing out of the human body does not mean the end of existence. God will provide the kind of house needed for eternal habitation. There is even an element of contrast in the use of the term "tabernacle," or tent, which describes the earthly dwelling, and the term "building," that is, a more permanent structure, which describes the eternal dwelling.

In verse 2 Paul indicated that while in this earthly house, which wears out from day to day, the believer looks with longing to the possession of the heavenly habitation, which will never wear out. He has the desire to receive that heavenly habitation immediately after death so that he will not go through a period of being a disembodied spirit. A believer's groaning in this earthly tent does not mean that he wants to be rid of the body and become simply a spirit (v. 4). Paul said that he did not want to be rid of this earthly tent in order to be an untented or unclothed spirit. Rather, he wanted to exchange this earthly tent which is subject to decay and death for an eternal house which will not be subject to decay and death. He wanted to put on his eternal body without being temporarily a disembodied spirit.

In verse 6 Paul spoke of the good courage which characterized his own attitude. While the believer is at home in this earthly body, there is a sense in which he is absent from the Lord; he does not see the Lord objectively, though by faith he walks in the presence of the Lord. In verse 8 Paul indicated that to be absent from this body means to be immediately at home with the Lord. This is the position which he presented in other places, namely, that to die means to lay aside the physical body but to be, as far as the spirit is concerned, in the immediate presence of Christ. Therefore, Paul indicated in verse 8 a willingness to lay aside this body even though it meant becoming temporarily a disembodied spirit in order that he might be immediately at home with the Lord. He was willing to be a disembodied spirit because he as a Christian made it his aim to be in that condition which would be pleasing to the Lord (v. 9). If the Lord's will means continuing in this physical body, that is all right; if it means laying aside this physical body and becoming a disembodied spirit until the time of the resurrection, that, too, is all right. The main thing is to be pleasing to God in the light of the fact that one day all men shall be called upon to stand the test of judgment before him (v. 10).

In summary fashion, then, we may organize the view which Paul sets out in this paragraph: (1) God has for our eternal habitation a body which will be the dwelling place of the spirit for eternity. It is related to the body which we occupy here in that it takes the place of this earthly body. We do not possess it now, but in the purpose of God it is ours. This present tense "we have" is used much in the same way in which in popular terminology we say that we *have* a home in heaven or we *have* an inheritance from God. Possession is reality, though reception waits for God's own time. (2) This body which we are to have is the one which God gives for the eternal dwelling place of the spirit. This recalls the 1 Corinthians 15 passage in which Paul sets out at length the fact that these frail bodies that we have in this world are not fit subjects for eternal dwelling and they must be changed before they can be fit subjects for eternal dwelling. The idea here is identical. (3) As Paul faces his prospects for the future, he sees before him two alternatives by way of which he might come to his eternal body. One way would be that of laying aside this body and becoming an unclothed (a disembodied) spirit until the resurrection. This is in line with 1 Thessalonians 4 and 1 Corinthians 15. The other way would be to continue in this life until the Lord's return and then by means of the instantaneous transformation discussed in 1 Corinthians 15 to put on the eternal body over this mortal one as one would slip a new robe on over an old robe, which old robe dropping away would leave him not an unclothed person but a newly clothed person. As Paul looks at these two ways by which people are to be changed for eternal habitation, the same two ways which he discussed in 1 Corinthians 15, he expresses a heart-longing to be changed by living until Christ comes and being transformed, rather than to be changed by death, disembodied state, and the resurrection of the body at the second coming of Christ. Even though that is his personal desire, there is something which is of greater importance than that, and that is the will of the Lord for Paul. So Paul says if it is the will of the Lord for him to lay aside this body and to be unclothed (a disembodied spirit) until the time of the resurrection, he is willing for that because it means that he will be in the immediate presence of Christ. Conscious relationship with his Lord does not stop, and he will be in that state doing that which is well pleasing to Christ. This interpretation of the passage is consistent with every other expression of Paul with reference to the resurrection of the body. Furthermore, it has the almost unanimous support of the commentaries everywhere recognized as the best.

Systematic Survey

Against the background of this interpretation of these basic New Testament passages on the resurrection, attention may be directed to an organized treatment of the subject. The fact of the resurrection is everywhere apparent in the New Testament. It is found in the teachings of Jesus as reflected in the gospels. It is found, too, in the preaching of the apostles as reflected and recorded in the book of Acts. It is found in the epistles of Paul, as well as other writers. Last of all, it is found in the book of Revelation.

The fact of the resurrection.—Jesus taught that the resurrection was to be experienced by men. In Matthew 12:41–42, in speaking of judgment on the wicked people of his own day, he said that men of Nineveh would be raised up in judgment as witnesses against the contemporaries of Jesus who rejected him and his message. He went on to say that these people of Nineveh repented when Jonah preached concerning God's judgment. Jesus' own generation, however, refused to repent even though he, the One greater than Jonah, had preached to them concerning the judgment of God. The emphasis of the passage for present purposes is the fact that Jesus spoke of the resurrection as being an element of future experience for the people of the time of Jonah.

Jesus spoke very definitely in the Gospel of John concerning the resurrection. In John 5:28–29 he spoke of the hour to come when "all who are in the tombs will hear his voice and will come forth" in the experience of resurrection. In similar fashion, in John 6:39–40, 44, and 54 he spoke of the resurrection "in the last day." In John 11:23 ff. Jesus accepted Martha's affirmation of faith that her brother Lazarus would be raised from the dead at the last day, but he went beyond that to teach an important lesson: Those who believe in him are so closely linked to the principle of life that even though physical death comes they go on in the experience of life on its most transcendent plane. This was no denial of the truth of the resurrection which Martha accepted. It was an endorsement of that truth plus an extended teaching based on it.

In John 14 Jesus spoke of his going away to prepare a place for his followers and of his coming again to receive them. One of the climactic statements in this connection is that in John 14:19, when Jesus said, regarding his resurrection, "Because I live, you also will live." All of these passages affirm Jesus' confidence in the resurrection as a fact in man's experience.

This emphasis of Jesus was continued by the apostles in

their preaching following his ascension. It is clear that one of the objections of the Sadducees to the preaching of the apostles was the fact that they were proclaiming the resurrection from the dead through Jesus (Acts 4:2). This meant that the dominion of death already had been invaded [25] and that in Jesus man could prove the doctrine of the resurrection.

This preaching of Peter and John as recorded in the Acts has an echo in the writings of the apostle Peter. In 1 Peter 1:3 faith in the resurrection of Jesus from the dead is affirmed; there is also confidence that all who belong to Jesus have an incorruptible inheritance reserved for them in heaven. On the basis of this verse only the hope of some manner of personal survival after death could be affirmed. When the passage is related to other passages in the New Testament, however, it appears that this hope in personal survival after death can be understood only in the hope of the resurrection from the dead.

Related to this area of Hebrew Christianity as found in the first chapters of Acts and in the writings of Peter is the Epistle to the Hebrews. Here, too, the resurrection is affirmed. In Hebrews 6:2 the resurrection is listed as one of the first principles or basic doctrines of the Christian faith. It is listed along with repentance, faith, baptism, eternal judgment, and other basic elements. No argument is given to prove the doctrine. It is simply listed as one of the accepted doctrines of the faith. In Hebrews 11:35 the resurrection is noted again in the reflection of the idea that those who were martyrs for their faith in God were worthy of a better resurrection. Again no elaboration of the passage is given. There is no comment as to whether or not martyrs actually receive a better estate in the resurrection. There is only the reflection of the idea among early Christians that those who were loyal to the point of death were worthy of some priority in the eternal experience of men.

[25] Cf. Cullmann, *Christ and Time, op. cit.*, pp. 235 ff.; Emil Brunner, *The Great Invitation* (London: Lutterworth Press, 1955), p. 130.

It is in the writings of Paul that the doctrine of the resurrection is presented at greatest length. Paul's faith in the resurrection is reflected in his preaching in such passages as Acts 23:6 and Acts 24:15. These passages are personal testimonies of Paul's belief in the resurrection. In his written work further emphasis is laid on the doctrine. (See on 1 Thess. 4:13–18 and 1 Cor. 15 above.)

Philippians 3:10–11 reflects confidence in the resurrection of Jesus as part of an experience that is available to men, and in Philippians 3:20–21 Paul looked to that time when Christ would fashion anew the body and make it conformable to the likeness of his own resurrection body. In 2 Timothy 2:11 Paul, in the shadow of death, affirmed his faith that just as he was to be joined with Jesus in the experience of his death even so would he be joined with him in the experience of resurrection.

Specific attention will be devoted later to the doctrine of the resurrection in Revelation 20. It must be noted at this point, however, that the fact of the resurrection is there endorsed and that the judgment scene in Revelation 20:11–15 has little meaning apart from the doctrine of the resurrection.

The agent of the resurrection.—The New Testament teaching regarding the agent of the resurrection is important because of the question raised by many in the New Testament day (and since) as to the "how" of the resurrection. The most direct approach to this problem is Paul's answer in 1 Corinthians 15:35–50. For him the answer was simply that the resurrection becomes reality through the power of God. This idea was not original with Paul. In the teachings of Jesus the resurrection is always related directly to the power of God. In Matthew 22:23–33, Jesus said that the Sadducees' error in rejecting the doctrine was due in part to the fact that they did not understand the power of God.

Once the power of God is added to the phenomenon, the

impossibility is removed from it. This is true of all the miraculous in the New Testament, and it is no less true of the miracle of resurrection. God's being the agent in the resurrection is the major element in the writings of Paul. In 1 Thessalonians 4:14 there is the statement that when Jesus comes, God will bring with Jesus those believers who have died prior to his coming. In Romans 4:17 it is God who gives life to the dead, and in Romans 8:11 it is God who will quicken men's mortal bodies so that they can never be subject to death again. In the Corinthian correspondence God is the agent in the resurrection in such passages as 1 Corinthians 6:14; 2 Corinthians 1:9; 4:14; and 13:4.

There are passages in the New Testament which refer to Christ as the agent in the resurrection. These in no way conflict with the teaching that God is the agent in the resurrection. The idea of the oneness of Father and Son is most pronounced in the Gospel of John. It is only natural then that in John 5:25–29 and John 6:39–40, 44, and 54 Jesus spoke of himself as the One who would raise the dead in the last day. Paul reflected this idea in 1 Corinthians 15:20–28 and Philippians 3:20–21. It is in Christ that all will be made alive; it is Christ who will fashion anew the physical body, making it like his glorious body. In the Matthew 12:41–42 passage no agent of the resurrection is expressed. The statement is simply made that the men of Nineveh will be raised up in judgment. All of this underscores the fact that the doctrine of the resurrection was no problem to Jesus and to Paul. They related it to the power of God, believing that God has the power to make the resurrection a reality.

All to be raised.—The resurrection of all men is an accepted doctrine. A review of the confessions of faith of the major branches of the Christian religion reveals a general acceptance of the doctrine of the resurrection. This belief is basic in the Augsburg Confession (Lutheran), the Westminster Confession (Presbyterian), the Thirty-nine Articles (Church of England), the New Hampshire Confession (followed by a majority of Baptist groups), the Reform Episcopal Articles of the American Episcopal Church, and while not positively stated, it is implied in the Articles of Religion of the Methodist Church.[26] This affirmation of faith in the resurrection is in the resurrection of all men, both righteous and unrighteous. In commenting on the New Hampshire Confession of Faith, Mullins [27] speaks of faith in the view that at death the bodies of all people return to the earth but that all will be raised. He recognizes that little is taught in the Bible regarding the resurrection of the wicked apart from the fact itself.

The idea of the resurrection of righteous and unrighteous is found in Daniel 12:2: "And many of those who sleep in the land of the dust will awake, some to everlasting life and some to everlasting shame and contempt." Paul's view of the resurrection of both the just and the unjust is affirmed in Acts 24:15. It may be that 2 Thessalonians 1:7–10 includes the idea of the resurrection of the unrighteous. Certainly it speaks of punishment for the unrighteous in relationship to the second coming of Christ and of judgment. Revelation 20:12–13 is understandable only in relationship to the resurrection of the unrighteous.

In the teachings of Jesus the resurrection of the unrighteous is clearly stated in John 5:28–29, and it is rather definitely implied in such passages as Matthew 7:21–23; 13:36–42; 16:24–27; and 25:31–46.

The time of the resurrection.—One of the most important

[26] "Christ did truly rise again from the dead, and took again his body, with all things appertaining to the perfection of man's nature, wherewith he ascended into heaven, and there sitteth until he return to judge all men at the last day." These statements of faith may be found in Philip Schaff, *The Creeds of Christendom* (New York: Harper & Brothers, 1919).

[27] Edgar Young Mullins, *Baptist Beliefs* (Philadelphia: Judson Press, 1951), p. 59.

problems relative to the New Testament doctrine of the resurrection is the time of the resurrection. Always the resurrection was spoken of as something in the future. Second Timothy 2:18 mentions certain ones who were in error in saying that the resurrection already had passed. Interpreters are divided on what Paul had in mind in this statement. Some understand it as a reference to the idea that all that one receives for eternity he receives at the point of death so that he does not look to any future resurrection of the body at the time of the second coming of Christ. Others relate it to the idea that the resurrection referred only to a spiritual awakening of the individual so that through regeneration he is lifted to a higher plane of life and that this "spiritual resurrection" is all that is involved in the doctrine of the resurrection. Regardless of the specific problem with which this passage dealt, Paul would have rejected either view suggested. A spiritual resurrection would be, in his thinking, no resurrection of the body at all. Likewise he would reject the idea that the individual at death passes to his eternal state in such way that the body is never to be raised from the dead. This, too, to Paul would be no resurrection at all. He sees God's total purpose for man embraced in redemption of the entire man, body and spirit. This total purpose cannot be realized without the resurrection of the body and its transformation, so it can never again be subject to death. This belief finds its New Testament beginning in the teachings of Jesus (John 5:28–29; 6:39–54; and 11:24–25). It is also found in Paul's writings, as in his statement in Romans 8:23 about waiting for the redemption of the body. This is not a matter of waiting for the redemption of the body at death. It is rather the waiting for the redemption of the body in relationship to the consummation of God's purpose for man in the consummation of his purpose for the entire created universe (Rom. 8:18–25). The power of the cross reaches to the total result of sin in man and in the universe itself. When the consummation of God's purpose for the universe is realized, a part of that consummation will be the resurrection of the dead.

The future nature of the resurrection is specifically related by Paul to the time of the second coming of Christ. The entire argument of 1 Thessalonians 4:13–18 is to the effect that the resurrection will become reality when the Lord returns to the earth. In the same manner, the entire argument in 1 Corinthians 15:20–58 relates the resurrection to the second coming of Christ. Second Thessalonians 1:7 appears, too, to relate the consummation of resurrection and judgment to the time of the second coming of Christ.

One other question must be faced as to the problem of the time of the resurrection: are the righteous and the unrighteous to be raised at the same time? The confessions of faith of the major groups in the Christian religion recognize only one resurrection, which is to come to all men at the time of the second coming of Christ. This is true, also, of the commentaries which have been cited. It must be recognized, however, that there are some groups (and they are not limited to any particular denomination) which do not share this view. They hold that the righteous are raised from the dead at one time and the unrighteous at another. In the Appendix of this book is a sketch which relates different views in eschatology one to another by several different approaches to the problem. For present purposes emphasis must be given to this particular phase of the subject.

Essential to the idea of two resurrections is an expectation that Christ will rule for a thousand years (the millennium) here in this world between the time of his second coming and the time of the final consummation of the world and the beginning of the eternal order. All the righteous who have died prior to the coming of Christ will be raised to share with him in the glory of that millennial reign, but the unrighteous will not be raised until the end of the thousand years. They will at that time be raised for judgment. The view has manifold variations according to the particular writer. While there are differences at specific points, it is set out most clearly in such works as those by Scofield,[28] Talbot,[29] Larkin,[30] and Ladd.[31]

These writers believe, generally, that the "first resurrection" is divided into two parts, the "rapture" and the "revelation," which are seven years apart, and relates only to believers. At the "rapture" Christ will come only to raise the righteous who have already died and to call out of the world the righteous who are still living. This is also called the "harvest." This calling of all of the righteous out of the world, including the taking from the earth of the Holy Spirit, leaves the world in the complete possession of evil for a seven-year period known as the "great tribulation." Those who are converted to the Christian faith and die during the seven-year period will be raised at the end of that period. This is called the "gleanings." The "harvest" and the "gleanings" are together considered the first resurrection.

This is the general view of Larkin, Talbot, and Scofield. Ladd disagrees to the extent that he does not divide the "rapture" and the "revelation." He holds that the second coming of Christ is to be one event at the close of the seven-year period of tribulation. The "second resurrection" comes at the end of the thousand-year reign of Christ on the earth. It, too, is divided into two parts but not at two separate times. In the "second resurrection" the righteous who became believers and died during the thousand years will be raised with the wicked

[28] C. I. Scofield (ed.), *The Scofield Reference Bible* (New York: Oxford University Press, 1945), pp. 1269, 1334, 1349–50, *et al.*

[29] Louis T. Talbot, *The Revelation of Jesus Christ* (Grand Rapids: Wm. B. Eerdmans Publishing Co., 1953), pp. 65–69, 230–38, *et al.*

[30] Clarence Larkin, *The Book of Revelation* (Philadelphia: Rev. Clarence Larkin Estate, 1919), pp. 32–34, 176–80, *et al.*

[31] George Eldon Ladd, *The Blessed Hope* (Grand Rapids: Wm. B. Eerdmans Publishing Co., 1956), pp. 71–167.

dead of all ages. This resurrection will be consummated in the "great white throne" judgment.

There is an almost limitless variety of detailed interpretation on the part of those who hold to this view. The starting point for this approach is Revelation 20:4–6. Those who hold the doctrine of two resurrections say this passage teaches that the righteous will be raised at one time and the unrighteous at another. In fact, for most interpreters who hold this view the resurrection of the wicked will take place one thousand and seven years after the resurrection of the righteous; the righteous are raised at the beginning of the great tribulation, which is followed by the one-thousand-year reign of Christ on the earth. The expression in the last part of verse 5, "the first resurrection," refers to the resurrection of the righteous, and the expression in the first part of verse 5, "the rest of the dead," refers to the resurrection of the wicked at the end of the millennium.

Those who reject the doctrine of two separate resurrections find difficulty with the point of departure of those who accept it. A basic principle of interpretation of the Scripture at all places is that the difficult and obscure passage must be interpreted in the light of the clear passages. This paragraph is one of the most difficult and obscure passages in all the Bible. A part of the problem is that this is the only place in the New Testament where two resurrections are mentioned. That does not mean that the doctrine is to be ruled out on that basis. One clear statement in the New Testament that the righteous are to be raised at one time and the wicked a thousand years later would be sufficient. But nowhere else in the Bible is there such a statement, and this passage can hardly be called clear. Interpretations of it range from the idea that both resurrections are literal to the idea that both resurrections are symbolic. In between is the idea that one is symbolic and the other is literal.

Already reference has been made to those who hold that both resurrections are literal.[32] B. H. Carroll [33] insists that both expressions refer to souls, not to bodies. The first resurrection is a symbol of the triumph of the Christian cause over the forces of evil; the souls of those who had died out of their loyalty to Christ are triumphant and live and reign with Christ for a thousand years. The expression "the rest of the dead lived not" is interpreted by Carroll as a reference to the souls of the wicked; during a brief period at the close of the millennium the forces of evil reassert themselves, and for a short time their cause appears to be victorious. Their seeming to be victorious, however, comes to an end with the coming of Christ and the complete defeat of evil. Carroll holds that there is not a word in these three verses which tells about the coming of Christ or a bodily resurrection. The New Testament doctrine of the resurrection, he holds, is fulfilled in Revelation 20:12–13.

Another interpreter who has something of this same idea is Lenski.[34] His understanding of the first resurrection seems to be the same as that of Carroll. He insists that souls and not bodies reign with Christ; at death the soul enters heaven and joins Christ in his kingly rule until his second coming. Lenski's view of the expression "the rest of the dead lived not until the thousand years were ended" differs from Carroll's. Lenski sees it only as a negative statement given by way of contrast to show the blessedness of the godly rule with Christ and the fact that this blessedness was denied those who died without Christ. Like Carroll he holds that the resurrection of all takes place in Revelation 20:12–13. He makes much of the Greek text in his interpretation, calling attention to the fact that the

[32] Ladd, Larkin, Scofield, and Talbot.

[33] B. H. Carroll, "The Book of Revelation," *An Interpretation of the English Bible* (New York: Fleming H. Revell Co., 1913).

[34] R. C. H. Lenski, *The Interpretation of St. John's Revelation* (Columbus: Wartburg Press, 1943), pp. 578–90.

Greek term throughout is the term for souls and to the fact that the verb translated "live" is the Greek verb which means to receive life on the very highest plane, not the Greek word generally translated "resurrection."

Still another variation is presented by McDowell.[35] McDowell joins others who hold that the millennium is a symbol of the period of history from the time of Christ's first coming and redemptive work until the time of his second coming in consummation. He understands the first resurrection to refer to the souls of the Christians who lived in the time of Nero and Domitian and who experienced persecution because of their Christian faith. He thinks that the term may refer in a general sense to all of Christ's people through the ages but that its particular reference is to those persecuted Christians who were loyal in Christianity's darkest hour. In this vision John sees these souls not dead as their bodies were put to death but alive and enjoying the triumphant reign of Christ.

The expression "the rest of the dead" McDowell understands to refer to all non-Christians, but he thinks that it, too, may by contrast with the martyrs have a specific reference to those who were identified by the mark of the beast as belonging to Domitian, who was attempting to destroy Christianity. These souls experienced no such blessedness as that experienced by the Christian dead, and their ultimate destiny is the lake of fire along with their leader, Satan.

Is it necessary to hold either that both resurrections in this passage are resurrections of the body or that both resurrections are resurrections of the soul? Can it be that there is a mixture of the symbolic and of the literal? Such a view has been suggested as possible in an earlier work.[36] The term "first res-

---

[35] Edward A. McDowell, *The Meaning and Message of the Book of Revelation* (Nashville: Broadman Press, 1951), pp. 190–95.

[36] Ray Summers, *Worthy Is the Lamb* (Nashville: Broadman Press, 1951), pp. 204–206.

urrection" and the term "second death" are both symbolic. The "second resurrection" and the "first death," which are not mentioned but which are implied, are to be understood as literal.

The New Testament teaches that when Christ comes, the dead will be raised. John used the term "resurrection" to describe the blessed experience of the martyrs. The New Testament also teaches the fact of physical death which means, among other things, a separation, a condition of being cut off from what in other circumstances has been a desirable life. John used the term "second death" as a symbol of the eternal separation from the blessings and fellowship with God which is otherwise known as hell. Thus, observe the following:

The "first resurrection" is a symbol of the triumph of the martyrs.	The "second resurrection" (not mentioned but implied) is the general resurrection.
The "first death" (not mentioned but implied) is physical death.	The "second death" is a symbol of eternal punishment in separation from the blessings of God.

When the entire book of Revelation is interpreted in the light of its historical setting, it seems certain that those described in verse 4 as reigning were the martyrs who lost their lives in that period of the persecution of the Christians. In the symbolism of the book, however, they were seen not to be defeated in death but to be triumphant with Christ. So glorious was their triumph that they were pronounced "blessed and holy," and their absolute freedom from the power of the second death is proclaimed. Their cause triumphed as certainly as Satan's cause was defeated.

The second passage used to support the doctrine of separate resurrections of the righteous and the wicked is 1 Thessalonians 4:16. The idea is that the statement "the dead in Christ will rise first" indicates that the wicked dead will be raised later. That, however, is not Paul's statement at all. Reference to the previous interpretation of the passage will show the sequence involved here. Paul said nothing whatever about the wicked dead because they were no part of the problem before him. He was speaking of two groups of believers and their relationship to the Lord's return, i.e., the believers who die prior to the Lord's return and the believers who still live when the Lord returns. He showed that they will share equally in the experience of the Lord's return. *First* the dead believers will be raised; *then* the living believers will be caught up to join that one glorious company forever. This is the sequence and the only one in the passage.

Another passage frequently used in support of the idea of separate resurrections is Matthew 24:37–41. The particular reference is to verses 40 and 41: "Then will be two in the field, one man is taken and one is left; two women grinding at the mill, one is taken and one is left." The passage is one in which Jesus was discussing his second coming. He was speaking of the fact that it will be unexpected, as in the days of Noah when men were so absorbed in the ordinary things of everyday life that they were not expecting anything unusual. Suddenly the judgment of God came and took them out of the world.

Those who find the possibility of two resurrections here admit that resurrection is not mentioned. They hold that this is a description of what they call the "rapture," when Christ comes to take believers out of the world and leave unbelievers in the world. They hold, further, that the righteous are raised but the unrighteous are left in the grave, just as the unrighteous who are living are left in the world. Those who deny this interpretation insist that this passage has to do only with the separation in judgment which will take place when Christ returns. It may also be noticed in objection that what happened in the day of Noah is the very opposite of what will happen when Christ comes to "rapture" his saints. In the days of Noah it was God's people who were left and the wicked who were taken.

In summary, it appears that the idea of separate resurrections for the righteous and the wicked a thousand years apart is not well-grounded in the Scripture. Two of the most specific statements about the resurrection are those previously cited, Daniel 12:2 and John 5:28–29. It is impossible to find any suggestion in these passages that there will be two separate resurrections. When Jesus spoke of the time of the resurrection of the righteous in John 6:39–40, 44, and 54, he said that he would raise up the one who was his "at the last day." When is the last day? Is it "the last day" or is it a thousand or a thousand and seven years before "the last day?" The conclusion is that the New Testament knows of only one resurrection—that of both the righteous and the wicked at the time of the second coming of Christ.

The resurrection body.—Investigation in one other area is necessary when dealing with the doctrine of the resurrection. That relates to the nature of the resurrection body. Caution is in order at this point because the writers of the New Testament were themselves cautious. There are phases of the subject which they discussed. There are other large areas where they were silent. In Matthew 22:23–33 Jesus taught that life in the resurrection will transcend the life which has been known here. It is clear that in the mind of Jesus the resurrection life will be for the believer life on the highest possible plane and for the unbeliever a life that is described by the term "judgment" (John 5:28–29).

The largest amount of material in the New Testament on this question is to be found in the writings of Paul. The passages have been interpreted previously. The bodies in the resurrection will be bodies made like Christ's resurrection body (Phil. 3:21). Paul's view was that whatever happened to Jesus in the experience of resurrection will happen to others, and since he believed that the body of Jesus was made alive and gloriously transformed, he believed that will take place in the experience of others as well. It is not Paul's view that individuals will be disembodied spirits for eternity. It is his view that the eternal state will be a bodily state ($\sigma \tilde{\omega} \mu a$ $\pi \nu \epsilon \nu \mu a \tau \iota \kappa \acute{o} \nu$), just as the state here has been a bodily state ($\sigma \tilde{\omega} \mu a$ $\psi \nu \chi \iota \kappa \acute{o} \nu$). There will be continuity between earthly bodies and heavenly bodies.

The transcendent nature of the body is seen in the illustration of the seed and the mature plant. Paul illustrated again by the relationship to Adam and to Christ: in this life there has been a body subject to death because of Adam; in the eternal life there will be a body not subject to death because of Christ. The body will be one adapted to eternal needs (2 Cor. 5:1–10). It will be a body that will take the place of the earthly one and will be the eternal dwelling place of the spirit.

All of this has to do with the resurrection body of the righteous, one made alive again, glorified so that it transcends this physical body and can never be subject to decay and death. What is to be said of the New Testament teaching concerning the problem of the resurrection of the wicked? Very little appears in the New Testament at this point beyond the affirmation of faith that both the righteous and the wicked will be raised. One might posit certain ideas by way of contrast, but the best course seems to be simply to leave the problem where it was left by the writers of the New Testament. Interpreters are practically unanimous in holding that the resurrection body of the wicked will also be one that is not subject again to death. It will be one which will be capable of experiencing the suffering which is in line with the wickedness which it has done.

One writer, however, does not see the resurrection body of

the wicked as one not subject to death. Larkin,[37] in strict accord with the literal interpretation which he follows, holds that the second death is as literal as the first (physical) death. It is his view that the wicked will be raised for judgment at the great white throne. When they have been judged worthy of death, they will die again and their eternal destiny in the lake of fire will be the destiny of a disembodied spirit. In this way Larkin seeks to avoid the idea of the annihilation of the body by the fire of hell. Others of his particular approach to interpretation and eschatology do not agree with him at this point. They hold that the wicked will have a deathless body capable of suffering punishment for eternity.

Paul believed that the body of Jesus was raised and transformed. He believed that all those who belong to Christ will be raised and transformed in the same way when Christ comes again and that only in this way can God's promise of victory over sin and death be fulfilled. So firm was his faith in this that he was willing to be a disembodied spirit because that would mean the presence, communion, and fellowship of Christ until the day when the ultimate experience of the resurrection of the body would be his. It is the Christian hope that believers shall one day know complete triumph in freedom from all that represents sin and weakness, as their bodies are raised and reunited with the spirit and enter fully into their eternal reward with Christ.

[37] Larkin, *op. cit.*, p. 194.

4.

The Second Coming

WHILE the term "second coming" is not found in the New Testament, it appeared early in Christian writings. It was used as early as the middle of the second century and perhaps earlier. Justin Martyr, in his First Apology (dated between A.D. 147 and 161), speaks of "two advents . . . the second, when, according to prophecy, He shall come from heaven with glory, accompanied by his angelic hosts, when also He shall raise the bodies of all men who have lived, and shall clothe those of the worthy with immortality and shall send those of the wicked, endued with eternal sensibility into everlasting fire with the wicked devils."[1] In other places in the writings of Justin the term ἡ δευτέρα παρουσία was used to refer to the coming of Christ at the end of the world in contrast to his earthly life and ministry which closed with the crucifixion, resurrection, and ascension.

The doctrine of the second coming occupied a very prominent place in the New Testament and in early Christian thinking. It was one of the teachings of Jesus which was most

[1] Justin Martyr, "The First Apology of Justin," *The Ante-Nicene Fathers*, eds. Alexander Roberts and James Donaldson (Grand Rapids: Wm. B. Eerdmans Publishing Co., 1956), I, 180.

precious to the followers left in the world when he ascended to the Father. Because of the fact that the material in the Gospels relates primarily to the earthly life and ministry of Jesus, the references to his second coming are relatively few. They are, however, sufficient and specific. Following the ascension of Jesus, because of his own promise to return and because of the promise of the heavenly messengers to those who witnessed the ascension, the followers of Jesus made much of the promise of his return. Their faith is reflected in the preaching and the writings of the apostles. This emphasis extended beyond the period of the writings of the New Testament; Christian literature of the second century reflects the acceptance of the teaching of the Lord's return and of the Christian hope in relationship to it.

In spite of the fact that the teaching has been precious to Christian hearts from the very beginning, great confusion has reigned historically and now reigns currently in the discussion of the doctrine. Doubtless this is true because of man's intense longing to know the details of the future of the world in relationship to the redemptive purposes of God. It is due in part, too, to the fact that little is given in the New Testament concerning the time of the second coming other than the idea of imminence; few details of what will take place at the Lord's return are given, other than the fact that it will mean resurrection, judgment, and the consummation of God's purpose for the world.

When men accept the New Testament teaching that when the Lord returns he will raise the dead, hold the final judgment of men, and establish the eternal order, there is general agreement and little confusion. When, however, men try to determine the events related to the Lord's return in more specific ways, confusion reigns. Because this has been the history of the doctrine, many Christians have neglected to give it the proper emphasis.

It is easy to take the approach that since so little can be known from the New Testament a Christian must be satisfied to leave all of that to the future and to concentrate on what Christ can mean to men in this world. While that may appear to be worthy, it leaves something lacking if it ignores what is in the New Testament regarding the second coming. On the other hand, it is evident that many have overemphasized the future. They have given an emphasis out of proportion to the place which the doctrine occupies in the New Testament. Undue emphasis has been given, too, in many instances, to an effort to determine the detailed events related to the Lord's return. It therefore appears all the more important that the subject be approached in the light of two questions: What are the New Testament passages which relate to the second coming? What do they reveal about the doctrine?

When the investigator attempts to make out a systematic program, great difficulty is involved. No one of the so-called systematic approaches to the subject is free of difficulties. Not one of them appears to have all the evidence clearly on its side. It appears, then, that the Lord must have meant for the teaching to be just as it is. He did not mean for men to have all of the details of his purpose for the future. If he had, surely the details would have been given in clearer fashion. That which Christians need to know, they do know: The Lord has promised to return to the earth; in connection with his return he will raise the dead and transform the living; he will exercise final judgment upon the deeds of men and their response to the offer of his mercy through his redemptive work; he will bring an end to the present world order and establish the eternal order for the glory of those who are his and the degradation of those who are not his. This much is clear. On these points most interpreters agree. It is when the details are pressed that difficulties become mountainous and confusion reigns.

A specific definition of the term "second coming" must be given. There have been various interpretations of the Lord's promise to return. Some have thought that the promise was fulfilled in the coming of the Holy Spirit at Pentecost. Others have seen fulfilment in the destruction of Jerusalem in A.D. 70. This was interpreted at a very early date as the coming of Christ in judgment upon the nation of Israel for their rejection of him as Messiah. It brought to an end their religious system, of which Jesus had been the fulfilment, though they had not accepted him as such. Still others find the Lord's promise to return to be related only to his coming to receive the believer at the point of death. When Stephen was stoned to death, he saw the living Christ *standing* ready to receive him (Acts 7:55). The emphasis in the Gospels, in Acts, in the Epistles, and in Revelation, however, is on a *personal, visible, and triumphant return of Christ to the earth to consummate the purpose of God in history and to usher in the eternal order.* It is in this sense that the term "second coming" will be used in this book.

The verb that is used most often in the New Testament for the Lord's return is ἔρχομαι. This word means literally "I come." It is the one that Jesus used in Matthew 24–25 when he spoke of the coming of worldly masters after a journey. He used these illustrations to speak of his own coming.

There are three noun forms which are used in the New Testament and which must appear as basic in this study. One is ἐπιφάνεια.[2] It comes from the verb ἐπιφαίνω, which means to show, to appear, to become visible. The noun was used by the Greek people in telling of the appearance of their gods to render aid to men in their need. It was also used in 2 Maccabees to show the presence and power of God with his people. The word is used once in the New Testament to refer to the first

[2] W. F. Moulton and A. S. Geden, *A Concordance to the Greek New Testament* (Edinburgh: T. and T. Clark, 1950), p. 374.

coming of Christ (2 Tim. 1:10). The word is used five times
in the New Testament to refer to the second coming of Christ
(1 Tim. 6:14; 2 Tim. 4:1, 8; 2 Thess. 2:8; Titus 2:13). In all
six uses it is commonly translated "appearing."

In 2 Thessalonians 2:8 ἐπιφάνεια is joined with another of the
basic nouns for the second coming, παρουσία. Here Paul spoke
of the triumph of Christ over all opposition and of his victory
over "the man of sin," whom he shall destroy with the brightness of his coming. The literal translation would be "by the
appearing of his coming."

Another word which is used in the New Testament for the
second coming is ἀποκάλυψις.[3] This noun is from the verb
ἀποκαλύπτω, which means literally "I uncover, I unveil, I reveal." In the King James Version the word is translated three
different ways. In 1 Peter 1:7 it is translated "appearing." In
1 Peter 1:13 the word is translated "revelation." The same
noun form is used in 1 Peter 4:13, and in 2 Thessalonians 1:7,
but in the King James Version it is translated as though it were
a verb. In Luke 17:30 the verb form is used. Again, in 1 Corinthians 1:7 the noun form is used. In this instance the King
James translation is "waiting for the coming of our Lord Jesus
Christ." A literal translation would be "waiting for the revelation of our Lord Jesus Christ." It seems that there can be no
question that all of these are references to the second coming.

A third word which is used (and it is the one which is used
most often) is παρουσία.[4] This noun is from the verb πάρειμι,
which means "I am beside" or "I am alongside." It is translated
"coming" in the King James, American Standard, and Revised
Standard versions. Many authorities prefer to translate it "presence." Both are good translations. It is the word which the
early Christian writers used in the term ἡ δευτέρα παρουσία,
"the second coming." It was used commonly of a visit which

[3] *Ibid.*, p. 92.
[4] *Ibid.*, p. 764.

any person would make to another, and it is in this way that the word is used in the New Testament. It will be found in this usage in Matthew 24:3, 27, 37, and 39.

Paul made much use of this word. He used it in 1 Corinthians 15:23 to refer to the resurrection which would be at the Lord's coming. He used it four times in 1 Thessalonians, and each time it has to do with the second coming of Christ (2:19; 3:13; 4:15; 5:23). He used the expression twice in 2 Thessalonians (2:1) and, as has been observed already, he joined it with ἐπιφανεία in 2:8.

Peter, too, used the word with reference to the Lord's coming or presence. It is found in 2 Peter 1:16 where it could possibly refer to the incarnation or to the second coming. In 2 Peter 3:4 and 3:12 it very clearly refers to the second coming. The word is also used with reference to the second coming in 1 John 2:28.

This review of terminology, particularly of nouns used, indicates a variety of expression but one basic idea. The appearing, the revealing, the coming, the presence of Christ—all of these terms speak of that glorious consummation of his purpose which is a part of Christian hope.

The Certainty of His Coming

One theme that runs throughout the preaching and writing of the apostles is the certainty of the Lord's return. It had its beginning in the teachings of Jesus himself and is reflected in all four of the Gospels. Sometimes it is a teaching which is definitely stated. At other times it is a teaching which was accepted by Jesus in making an argument or in presenting some other teaching. One of the earliest references is that found in Luke 12:39–40. Jesus was warning his disciples to be watchful for the coming of the Son of man. He referred to a house master whose house had been invaded by a thief. He said that if the master of the house had known when the thief was coming, he would have been watchful. He followed the story with an application: "Be you also ready, for in an hour that you think not, the Son of man comes." When Peter asked if Jesus meant that parable for them or for his disciples at large, Jesus answered with another story which seems to suggest that "Wherever the conditions are met, apply the story."

Another occasion when Jesus spoke of the certainty of his coming is recorded in Luke 17:22–37. The Pharisees had asked him when the kingdom of God would come. His answer to them was that the kingdom is an inner spiritual thing; it does not come with outward manifestations. Then to his disciples he spoke of the days that would come when they would desire to see his coming. The major emphasis in this passage is on the self-evident nature of the second coming: when it becomes reality, men will recognize it without having to be informed that it has taken place. However, it is important also that Jesus spoke definitely of his coming as a matter of certainty.

In Matthew 19:28 Jesus spoke in terms which assumed his second coming. Simon Peter had inquired about the future of the disciples, for they had given up much to become Jesus' followers. Jesus assured Peter that everyone who gives up anything in this life for the Lord will receive a hundredfold in return in the present, will receive everlasting life in the future, and when the Son of man sits upon his glorious throne in the consummation of God's purpose among men, his followers will share his glory with him.

Another example of Jesus' referring to his second coming is the passage which is recorded in Matthew 26:64 and Mark 14:62. The occasion was Jesus' trial before the Sanhedrin. When the high priest put Jesus under oath to say whether or not he was the Christ, the Son of God, Jesus answered, "I am." He followed this declaration with the statement that he would be vindicated in his claim to be the Son of God when he should come on the clouds of heaven and sit at the right hand of power. This claim to be the Son of God was sufficient to cause the high priest to call for a vote of the court on the matter of whether or not Jesus had blasphemed. Some interpreters understand this passage to be a reference to Jesus' work through his disciples while others understand it to be a reference to the second coming. It seems very difficult to eliminate the idea of the second coming because of the statement regarding his "coming in the clouds of heaven," a term used in the New Testament and by the early writers to refer to the coming of Christ.

On one notable occasion Jesus discussed the certainty of his second coming ín response to a question that was asked by his disciples. The passage is found in parallel in Matthew 24–25; Mark 13; and Luke 21:5–36. The disciples' question was related to the destruction of Jerusalem and to Jesus' coming at the end of the world. They asked the question in a way that indicated that in their minds the two events would be one; Jesus, however, answered in a way that indicated that they were in error and that the destruction of Jerusalem would be one thing and his coming at the end of the world would be another. It is difficult to determine exactly where he stopped talking about one event and started talking about the other. It appears, however, that in Matthew 24:29 to 25:46 the major emphasis was on his second coming. There can be no question as to the certainty in the mind of Jesus of that coming.

The certainty of the Lord's return was continued in the preaching of the apostles and in the written literature which came to be the New Testament. The first example is recorded in Acts 1:11. When Jesus had disappeared from the sight of the disciples, they became conscious of the presence of two men who stood beside them in gleaming apparel and said, "Galilean men, why have you taken your stand gazing into heaven? This Jesus, the One who has been received up from you into heaven, so shall come in the same manner in which you have seen him going into heaven." The passage gives information about the manner of the Lord's return, but the emphasis here is on the ringing certainty of the promise in immediate relationship to the Lord's ascension. He came from heaven on a redemptive mission. Having completed that redemptive mission here in the world, he returned to heaven there to carry on his priestly work of intercession until that day when he will fulfil his promise to return.

The same emphasis is reflected in Acts 3:20 in Peter's sermon following the healing of the lame man. Peter stressed the fact that Jesus was the anointed One of God, that he had been put to death, that he had been raised from the dead, and that through faith in him this miracle of healing had been brought about. He challenged his hearers to repent of what they had done in bringing Jesus to his death and told them that the time was coming when God would send Jesus Christ back to the earth to bring a consummation to his purposes.

This same theme is also reflected in Peter's epistles. In 1 Peter 1:13 he wrote of the grace that will be brought at the revelation of Jesus Christ. In 2 Peter 3:1-7 he wrote that there were those who deny the coming of Christ; they rather mocked at the idea. Many years had passed since the Lord's death, resurrection, ascension, and the promise of his return. He had not returned, so the enemies of the Christians were scoffing and asking when he would come. Peter, however, noted that God is not limited by concepts as men are (v. 8). The delay of the Lord's return is not to be interpreted as negligence on God's part but as a challenge for bringing others to know him while there is time for repentance (v. 9). Finally, he affirmed the certainty of the Lord's return (v. 10).

This idea of the Lord's return is reflected in other passages also. In Hebrews 9:28 there is the statement that Christ will appear a second time. In Hebrews 10:37 a word of encouragement is given: "Yet in a little while he who comes will come."

James reflects the certainty of the Lord's return and calls for patience in the light of the Lord's return (5:7). In verses 8 and 9 he speaks of it in terms of present reality as he says, "The judge stands at the door."

The certainty of the Lord's return is frequently found in the writings of Paul. The references are not limited to one particular part of his ministry but are found in his earlier as well as in his later epistles. There are several in 1 Thessalonians, one of the earliest writings. In 1:9–10 Paul referred to the way the Christian people of Thessalonica had turned from the worship of false gods to serve the living and genuine God and "to wait for his Son from heaven." In 2:19 he spoke of them as his hope and joy in both the presence and the coming of Jesus Christ, and in 3:13 and 5:23 he prayed that God would establish their hearts, that they might be blameless before God at the coming of the Lord Jesus. In 4:13–18 Paul spoke of the certainty of the second coming in relation to the Christian hope of resurrection.

In later writings the same emphasis may be noted. For instance, in Philippians 1:6 there is the assurance that since God has started a good work in the Philippians, he will bring it to completion in the day of Jesus Christ. In Philippians 1:10 Paul spoke of his prayer for the Philippians that they might be sincere and without offense until the day of Christ. In Philippians 3:20 he spoke of waiting for the coming of the Lord from heaven. In Colossians 3:1–4 Paul spoke of the union of the believer with Christ; he carried the idea beyond union with Christ in this life to union with him in his second coming. All these references speak specifically of the certainty of the Lord's return as a basic part of Christian faith in the earliest years of Christian history.

The Manner of His Coming

Many ideas that relate to the manner of the Lord's coming will be discussed elsewhere in relation to the time of his coming, the resurrection, judgment, consummation, etc. One thing which must be emphasized is that his coming will be *personal*. This note is found in Jesus' own teachings. It was emphatically promised in the words of the divine messengers in Acts 1:11, "this same Jesus." In this verse the Greek bears striking force at the point of personal identity.

The personal idea is underscored, too, in 1 Thessalonians 4:16 in the statement, "the Lord himself will descend." This is the use of the Greek third personal pronoun in the nominative case for striking emphasis: "himself the Lord" is the One who will descend. The personal idea may be found in all of the promises of the Lord's return. Indeed, the promises of his return apart from the personal element would have had little meaning to those early Christians. It was this which they cherished as much as the complete victory for the cause of God among men.

The manner of the Lord's coming will also be *mysterious*. The Greek of Acts 1:11 can hardly be translated into smooth English. This is the expression: "Thus will come what manner you saw him going into heaven." The Greek term translated "what manner" is ὅν τρόπον. Wherever it is used it speaks of exactness. Here it would mean that the manner in which Jesus will return to the earth will be the same manner in which he went away. How far is this idea to be pressed? Does it refer to the cloud which took him away? It would appear that Jesus was first raised up from the earth by some unseen power and that a cloud then came under him (literally, the cloud received' under him) so that he could not be seen by the disciples (v. 9). They continued to watch, and when the cloud had disappeared, Jesus, too, had disappeared. There is much mystery about this. The passage may mean that Jesus will return in exactly this way. It may, however, mean only that his coming will be as mysterious and as difficult to explain as was his ascension. The clouds veiled his ascension; the clouds will unveil his return.

Another New Testament emphasis on the manner of the Lord's coming is that of *suddenness.* In Matthew 24:29 Jesus spoke of the suddenness or immediacy of the events related to his coming. In his illustrations in Luke 17:26–30 the idea of startling suddenness is apparent. Jesus emphasized this idea, too, in all of the stories which he told in Matthew 25 to illustrate the matter of preparedness in relation to the Lord's return.

The idea of suddenness was stressed by Paul in 1 Thessalonians 5:3: "When they say peace and safety, then sudden destruction comes upon them as travail upon a woman with child." All of the emphasis on this idea would seem to make it clear that the Lord's coming will be such that men cannot determine it beforehand. Even when the disciples asked for signs that would help them, Jesus gave them only teachings which would point up the importance of being ready for it whenever it came.

Another note relative to the manner of the second coming might be found in the word *triumphant.* Jesus' coming is spoken of as a glorious event in the consummation of God's purpose among men. Specifically it is mentioned as an event which will mean rest for those who belong to the Lord and punishment for those who have rejected him. Second Thessalonians 1:5–10 presents this idea. When Christ comes to be glorified, he will bring rest to his people, but his coming will mean a fire of vengeance upon those who know not God and who have not been obedient to the gospel of Christ. They shall be banished from the Lord's presence. It is certain that the coming of Christ includes the triumphant completion of God's purpose in this world.

In this triumphant return the Lord will be accompanied by those who have died trusting in him. In 1 Thessalonians 4:14 this idea is presented as a large part of the glorious experience of the Lord's return. The Christians at Thessalonica were to be encouraged in the realization that the Christians who had died prior to the Lord's return would return with him in the same spiritual state which they had known from death to the second coming. Their bodies will be raised to become the undying and eternal dwelling place of the spirit. The believers who are still in the world shall be caught up to welcome him. How dramatic is the contrast with his first coming! When he came as a babe in Bethlehem, he was welcomed by his mother and by Joseph and the limited number to whom the announcement was given. When he comes the second time, only God can estimate the number who will welcome him! His first coming was a very humble event. His second coming will be too glorious for man's words to describe. Only the event itself will be sufficient for an understanding of its glory.

The Time of His Coming

From the days of the disciples to the present there has been no part of the doctrine of the Lord's second coming that has created more interest than the question of the time of his coming. This has been true in spite of the fact that so little can definitely be known about the time of the Lord's return. The best starting place for a discussion is a reminder of Jesus' statement in Matthew 24:36 that the day of the second coming was a thing which was known only to the eternal God. Jesus said that the knowledge of the time of the Lord's return was a thing which was known neither to man nor to angels.

Some of the ancient Greek manuscripts of Matthew include the expression "neither the Son" as it is recorded in Mark 13:32. Jesus, in the days of his flesh, did not know the exact time of the second coming. If he did not know and if the angels had been denied that knowledge and if no one up to Jesus' time had been given that knowledge, it appears that God meant for the exact time to be unknown.

Jesus further emphasized this idea in Acts 1:7, when on the

occasion of his last appearance to his disciples he was asked again if it was his plan to restore the kingdom to Israel at that time. The disciples shared with their contemporaries the dream that one day they would have a nation of their own. They would no longer be ruled by Rome; their land would take its place among the nations of the world as had ancient Israel under David and Solomon. It may be that there were among Jesus' disciples those who hoped that he would become a reformer like Judas Maccabeus and lead in a revolt against Rome. One of Jesus' disciples was named Simeon the Zealot; his name most likely shows his association with the movement which reached such strength in A.D. 66 that it caused a revolt against Rome.

Oscar Cullmann [5] has given consideration to the possibility that some of the other disciples were of the same thinking. His suggestion that "Iscariot" is a Hebrew transcription of the Latin *sicarius* is most stimulating. To the Romans, the *sicarii* were the "knife men" who led the revolt against Rome. The description fits Judas. Further, Jesus named James and John "the thunderstorm boys"! Simon Peter was called Simon Bar-Jonah; the name is interpreted as being Simon, son of John, though the short form "Jonah" is not so used elsewhere. Simon *barjona* could mean, however, Simon "the terrorist"!

Jesus stopped such questioning once for all when he said, "To know times or seasons which the Father has placed in his own authority is not yours." The expression "his own" is very emphatic. Jesus told the disciples to be looking for power for witnessing rather than seeking knowledge about an earthly kingdom. That power they would receive when the Holy Spirit came upon them.

If man cannot know the definite time of the Lord's return, what can he know about the time of the Lord's return? This

[5] Oscar Cullmann, *The State in the New Testament* (New York: Charles Scribner's Sons, 1956), pp. 15–17.

appears to be the proper place for treating a section of the teachings of Jesus which was given in response to the question of the disciples about the time of the Lord's return. The passage is that previously cited in the Synoptic parallels (Matt. 24–25; Mark 13:1–37; Luke 21:5–36). It is one of the most difficult passages in the New Testament.[6] It was not given to satisfy curiosity about the future but for a threefold purpose: (1) to safeguard from misconception; (2) to restrain from impatience; and (3) to stimulate continuous watchfulness and faithfulness to the task of witnessing for Christ.

In this passage Jesus was discussing the destruction of Jerusalem which took place in A.D. 70 as a symbol of his own coming in judgment upon the world. The transition from one to the other was very natural. It was so natural, in fact, that it is impossible to tell positively where the line of division is to be placed, i.e., where Jesus stopped talking about the destruction of Jerusalem and began talking about the second coming and the end of the world. He told his disciples that Jerusalem was to be destroyed. He told them definitely and boldly that he himself would return in judgment upon the world. He told them clearly that these two events were *not* one and the same. He exhorted his followers to be expectant in their attitude toward his coming and to be ready for his return. He did not tell them when it would take place.

The setting of the passage is most important. This conversation took place on Tuesday afternoon of the week of Jesus' crucifixion. As he went out from the Temple with his disciples, they called his attention to the beauty of the Temple build-

---

[6] How much confusion and controversy has marked the discussion of this passage is reflected in G. R. Beasley-Murray's excellent book and bibliography on Mark 13:1–37, *Jesus and the Future* (London: Macmillan and Co., Ltd., 1954). See also Feuillet, A. "Le Sens du Mot Parousie dans L'Evangile de Matthieu," *The Background of the New Testament and Its Eschatology*, eds. W. D. Davies and D. Daube (Cambridge: Cambridge University Press, 1956), pp. 261–80.

ings. He must have startled them when he said, "I tell you there will not be left here one stone upon another which will not be thrown down" (Matt. 24:2). That silenced the disciples for a while. Even Simon Peter was quiet as they went out from the Temple, down the hill, across the brook Kidron, and over the Mount of Olives on their way to Bethany to spend the night.

Near the top of the Mount of Olives was a place where the people who walked from Jerusalem to Bethany stopped to rest after climbing the hill. Apparently it was there that the question came from the disciples. As they looked back toward the west, the descending sun caught the white stone and gold of the Temple buildings and presented them in a glow which must have been breathtakingly beautiful. Then the disciples, led by Peter, asked Jesus, "Tell us when shall these things be, what shall be the sign of your coming and of the end of the world?"

It appears that the disciples presented the two questions as a unit. Perhaps they could not think of the world's continuing beyond the destruction of the Temple. Ancient Roman appreciation for the Colosseum is reflected in the often-quoted statement, "While stands the Colosseum, Rome shall stand, and while Rome stands, the world; when falls the Colosseum, Rome shall fall, and when Rome falls, the world." The Romans could not imagine history beyond so devastating a thing as the destruction of Rome and the Colosseum. The Jewish people could not imagine history beyond so devastating a thing as the destruction of Jerusalem with its magnificent Temple.

However, in his answer Jesus separated the two. He explained to the disciples that the destruction of Jerusalem was one event which was destined to come and that his return at the consummation of God's purpose for the world was another. The two events were related only in the sense that the one illustrated and preceded the other, i.e., the destruction of

Jerusalem would precede the destruction at the end of the world and could be used to illustrate that destruction and judgment. The time sequence between the two was given only in that general way.

Beginning in Matthew 24:4 Jesus warned his disciples against being led astray by false reports. There would be occasions, such as the destruction of Jerusalem, when people would be disturbed in their thinking, but they were not to become hysterical (v. 6); they were to realize that those events did not mean the end of the world. As history unfolded, it would be inevitable that nation would rise against nation; there would be wars, famines, and natural calamities, but these would be simply an example of the travail which would be realized when the ultimate consummation would come. Jesus spoke of difficulties which his disciples would encounter in the days of turmoil; many would arise as false prophets in an attempt to lead people astray from the truth of Christ (v. 11 ff.). In all of these things, however, victory would not go to the opposition. The gospel of the kingdom was destined to be preached to the entire inhabited earth before the end should come. This prophecy may refer to the preaching of the apostles before A.D. 70. It is destined, of course, to be fulfilled in a much greater way before the second coming.

Jesus spoke specifically in verse 15 and following of the destruction that was to come upon Jerusalem. He made reference to the desecration of the Temple by the presence of the ancient Gentile ruler mentioned in Daniel and related it to the coming of the Roman general Titus and his defilement of the very Temple itself. The parallel in Luke 21:20–24 is most helpful at this point. There Jesus gave instructions as to the conduct of the people of Jerusalem when that destruction did take place. They were to flee for safety to the mountains. The ones who observed the approaching Romans from the top of a house were not to go downstairs to get material possessions. Rather,

111

they were to flee over the flat roof tops of the houses, escape over the walls of the city, and find security in the mountains. Ancient historians record that many escaped Jerusalem in exactly this way when destruction came.

In Matthew 24:19 and following Jesus spoke of the hardship that people would experience: the agony of expectant mothers and mothers with babies in arms and the difficulty of travel if the destruction should come in winter. Perhaps he made a very subtle thrust at a lingering legalism in the minds of his disciples when he said, "Pray you that your flight be not on a sabbath." On a sabbath the good, obedient Hebrew could travel only about three-fifths of a mile. That would not be enough to reach safety if the destruction came on a sabbath! Jesus spoke of the tremendous destruction in connection with this period of Israel's history which, if it had been continued, would have meant the destruction of all the Hebrew people. In the providence of God, however, that was not to be permitted (v. 22).

In Matthew 24:23 Jesus pointed out that at this time of turmoil there would be many who would be looking for God's Messiah to intervene and deliver them. So he said, "If anyone says to you, 'Look, here is the Christ,' you are not to believe it." Many would arise and claim to be the deliverer, but Jesus' followers were to understand, having been warned ahead of time, that these would be false prophets. If someone should report that Christ had come and was out in the wilderness, they were not to go seek him; if someone should report that he had come and was in the secret room, they were not to believe it. Jesus illustrated the self-evident nature of his coming in verse 27. When lightning flashes in the east, even in the west it is so evident that people do not have to be told that lightning has flashed in the east. He also illustrated by a figure commonly observed: when there are vultures wheeling in the sky, it is a self-evident matter that a body will be found.

So Jesus told his disciples that they were not to be deceived into believing that the destruction of Jerusalem, tragic as it was, meant the coming of the Messiah and the end of the world.

Up to this point Jesus' major emphasis seems to have been the answer to the first question of the disciples regarding the destruction of Jerusalem, "When will these things be?" Beginning with Matthew 24:29; Mark 13:24; and Luke 21:25, however, the major emphasis appears to be on Jesus' answer to the second part of the disciples' question, that relating to the second coming and the end of the world. Caution is in order at the point of trying to make an exact division of the material. If the division is made at Matthew 24:29, some difficulty will be encountered due to the fact that verse 34 appears to apply to the destruction of Jerusalem and perhaps also to the second coming of Christ. If, however, the division is made after verse 34, there is the difficulty of explaining verses 29–33 in connection with the destruction of Jerusalem. The best approach appears to be that in the entire discourse Jesus was foretelling in the beginning the destruction of Jerusalem and at the conclusion his second coming with the general judgment of mankind and the division of the good from the bad. The middle part of the discourse may be understood as a transition from the one to the other so that some of the discussion in each section may apply to the other section. While some parts refer exclusively to one event or the other, it is certainly clear that the destruction of Jerusalem gradually fades from the picture so that from 24:37 to the end of the discourse it has disappeared completely and nothing remains in view except the second coming and judgment.

One of the most pronounced difficulties in the passage is the use of the word "immediately" in Matthew 24:29. The problem is that Jesus had been very careful to explain to his disciples that the destruction of Jerusalem would not be the same thing as the judgment upon the world at the time of his second coming. He had been careful to explain that one may illustrate the other or there may be similar events in one or the other, but he had been definite that they would be two separate events. Then in this statement he appears to change, at least to the point of indicating that the second coming would follow immediately after the destruction of Jerusalem. According to Lenski,[7] some interpreters have attempted to explain the word to mean "suddenly." Carroll follows that interpretation; the statement would then read, "The sun will be immediately darkened." [8] This interpretation finds in the Greek word εὐθέως an adverbial force in relationship to the verb "darkened."

If this is the correct interpretation, Jesus would be making no comment on a temporal relationship between the destruction of Jerusalem and the second coming other than to say that the second coming would follow the destruction of Jerusalem (by how many years would not be indicated) and that it would come with startling suddenness. This idea of suddenness is, of course, found often in the New Testament. This interpretation may be strengthened by the fact that neither Mark nor Luke uses the word "immediately." While this is an appealing interpretation, it cannot be completely satisfying in the light of the total passage.

How, then, is the relationship of the two events as Jesus looked at them and discussed them to be explained? Ellicott [9] thinks that the answer is partially due to God's measurement of time rather than man's measurement of time, i.e., "a thousand years are as one day" (2 Peter 3:8). He thinks, too, that a part of the answer is due to facing honestly the statement

---

[7] R. C. H. Lenski, *The Interpretation of St. Matthew's Gospel* (Columbus: Wartburg Press, 1943), p. 947.

[8] B. H. Carroll, "The Four Gospels," *An Interpretation of the English Bible* (New York: Fleming H. Revell Co., 1916), pp. 288–89.

[9] Charles John Ellicott, *Commentary on the Whole Bible* (Grand Rapids: Zondervan Publishing House, 1954), VI, 149.

which Jesus made in Mark 13:32 and Matthew 24:36 that the exact time of the end was not known by the Son; it was known only by the Father.

Jesus looked at the two events as poets and prophets speak of some future events. Two lofty mountain peaks in the distance may appear to be immediately joined, or they may seem to be growing one out of the other, although in reality there may be many miles and many lesser peaks between them. In a painting on canvas there appears to be, on a level surface, flowers and a house. Beyond the house there are trees. Beyond the trees tower the mountains. Beyond the mountains there are the clouds in the sky. The painting is all on one surface, but at the same time it is obvious that the artist had in mind a depth perspective which would push one far beyond the other. In some such way Jesus looked at the judgment of God on Jerusalem and at the judgment of God on the world. The two were not one and the same, and yet there were many similar things in both of them.

Broadus [10] says that the expression "those days" is *naturally* but not *necessarily* related to the tribulation of verses 19–22. He appears to say that Jesus may have in mind a transition from tribulation of the days of the destruction of Jerusalem to tribulation of the days related to the coming of Christ and the end of the world.

Whatever the understanding of the word "immediately," the authorities are practically unanimous in holding that Jesus speaks in symbols or illustrations when he refers to the darkening of the sun and the failure of the moon and the stars to give their light. This apocalyptic usage was familiar to Jesus' followers from their knowledge of similar expressions in Old Testament usage, such as Isaiah 13:9–10; Ezekiel 32:7–8; Joel

[10] John A. Broadus, "Commentary on the Gospel of Matthew," *An American Commentary on the New Testament* (Philadelphia: American Baptist Publication Society, 1886), p. 490.

2:1–2, 10–11, 30–31; Amos 8:9; and Zephaniah 1:14–16. The coming of Christ in judgment to bring an end to the world order and to establish the eternal order will be in every way a world-shaking event.

In Matthew 24:30 Jesus stated that in connection with such an event there would appear "the sign of the Son of man in heaven." There has been much speculation as to exactly what this sign will be. The best interpretation appears to be that it will be nothing other than the Son of man himself appearing in all his glory and majesty. This is in agreement with the statements in Mark 13:26 and Luke 21:27. In all three accounts it is indicated that the Son of man will come on the clouds of heaven with power and great glory. This coming on the clouds is understood by most interpreters to mean his coming on a cloud as he went away on a cloud in his ascension (Acts 1:9).

Several have suggested, however, that the picture of his coming on a cloud speaks only of the mysterious element involved. Gloege [11] is representative of this view. The suggestion is that as a cloud veiled the ascension of Christ so a cloud will unveil the invisible Lord in his return to the earth. His ascension was a matter of mystery and veiling; his second coming will be a matter of revealing or unveiling. His coming will mean the gathering of his people unto himself (Matt. 24:31), the separation of the righteous from the wicked (Matt. 24:40–41), and the final judgment, which will consign the wicked to eternal punishment and introduce God's people to the supreme joy of their eternal reward (Matt. 25:31–46).

Jesus' parable of the fig tree in Matthew 24:32–33 illustrates something of the self-evident nature of the Lord's return. He had illustrated by the example of the lightning which flashes in the east and is seen in the west. In this parable he said that

[11] Gerhard Gloege, *Das Reich Gottes im Neuen Testament* (Leipzig: Borna, 1928), pp. 178–90.

when the fig tree puts forth its leaves, people know that summer is near; when men see the Son of man coming on the cloud of heaven with power and great glory, they will know that the end of all things is near.

Jesus' statement in verse 34, "This generation will not pass away until all these things are accomplished," has led to a great variety in interpretation. If it refers specifically to the destruction of Jerusalem, there is no real problem. This is the view of Bruce [12] and Smith.[13] This discourse was spoken about A.D. 30; the destruction of Jerusalem came about A.D. 70, or within the lifetime of many who were then living. If, however, the statement applies to the second coming of Christ, a problem is involved. Nineteen hundred years have passed and still the fulfilment has not been realized.

Many interpretations have been suggested. Some interpreters have understood the word "generation" to carry the idea of race. They understand that Jesus said that his coming would be within history while the human race is still on earth. This is perhaps an oversimplification and a most questionable interpretation. Others have understood "generation" to have a qualitative significance with reference to wicked men; when Jesus comes, there will still be wickedness and wicked men in the world. That, too, appears to be an oversimplification.

Lenski [14] holds that the word refers particularly to the Jews, who in their wickedness were rejecting Jesus when he was in the world and who will continue to do so. Carroll,[15] too, holds that the reference is to the Jews and that it predicts their continuance as a race; however, his view of the necessity of the conversion of the Jewish race antecedent to the millennium

[12] A. B. Bruce, "The Synoptic Gospels," *Expositor's Greek Testament* (Grand Rapids: Wm. B. Eerdmans Publishing Co., n.d.), I, 296.
[13] David Smith, *Commentary on the Four Gospels* (New York: Doubleday, Doran and Company, Inc., 1928), I, 418.
[14] Lenski, *op. cit.*, pp. 952–53.
[15] Carroll, *op. cit.*, pp. 304–305.

would not permit him to share the idea of the Jews' rejection of Christ until the time of his return. Contrarily, some have understood "generation" to have a qualitative sense with reference to Christian people. Those who follow that view understand that Jesus said his people would not be conquered by evil, but that there would always be Christians in the world. But none of these interpretations fit well the natural meaning of generation.

The most satisfactory interpretation seems to be that Jesus had reference to the principle [16] about which he had been talking—violence, turmoil, agony, false rumors of his coming, and the continued preaching of his word wherever men are found. Every generation since his time has seen these signs fulfilled in principle. As far as these signs are concerned, the coming could have been in any generation. The fact that he has not come yet is evidence only that the fulness of God's purpose in the world has not yet been realized; his coming will not be until that purpose is realized. The time and the purpose have not been revealed to men.

Although exegetes and theologians have wrestled long and earnestly with the statement of Jesus that not even the Son knows (Matt. 24:36; Mark 13:32), it must be understood that Jesus is not here setting forth a commentary on the limitation of his human consciousness. He is pointing out the impossibility of man's determining the end by showing that such knowledge is withheld from both the Son and the angels. It is a secret reserved for the Father alone. Strack and Billerbeck [17] quote Rabbi Jochanan, who held that God does nothing which he does not discuss with the higher family, that is, the angels. According to rabbinical tradition, however, the knowledge of

[16] Cf. Broadus, op. cit., p. 492.
[17] Hermann Strack and Paul Billerbeck, "Das Evangelium nach Matthaus," Kommentar zum Neuen Testament aus Talmud und Midrash (Munich: C. H. Becksche Verlagsbuchhandlung, 1924), I, 961.

the time of the end of the world was hidden even from the angels. Rabbi Schimeon understood Isaiah 63:4 to mean that God had reserved knowledge of the day of vengeance for himself and had not shared it even with the ministering angels. If from the Son and the angels the knowledge has been withheld, all men must be content without it.

In Matthew 24:37–41 Jesus spoke again of the fact that the coming of the Son of man would be when the world was not expecting it and that it would mean judgment upon men. He used as an illustration the experience of the people of the day of Noah. People in that day were eating, drinking, marrying, and giving in marriage until the day that Noah entered the ark; they ignored impending judgment until the flood came and took them away. The emphasis appears to be that they were so involved in the ordinary things of everyday life that they were not expecting anything unusual. Even though Noah preached to them of God's judgment, even though every blow of his hammer was a warning that judgment was coming, they were so involved in ordinary affairs that they paid no attention to the coming judgment of God. With dramatic suddenness it fell upon them and took them out of the world. Jesus said that that is the way it will be when the Son of man comes. He will come suddenly upon those engaged in the everyday affairs of life, and his coming will mean separation in judgment.

Following that dramatic statement, Jesus told several other stories which point up either one or both of these lessons: (1) Be ready for his coming; (2) Be busy at the task assigned until he shall come. The first illustration in Matthew's account is that of the parable of the master of the house (Matt. 24:43–44). It is a story which illustrates one thing—watchfulness. The master of the house did not know when the thief was coming; hence his house was robbed. Jesus concluded the story by saying, "You also be ready, for in an hour when you are not expecting it the Son of man will come."

His second illustration is of a master and his servants (Matt. 24:45–51). The master assigned certain household responsibilities to his servant. If, when the master returns from whatever journey he may have taken, he finds the servant discharging his responsibility, he will bless the servant by giving him a position of greater honor; if, on the other hand, the servant proves to be evil in his heart and takes advantage of his master's absence, he will be surprised in the midst of his disobedience by the return of his master, who will punish him severely for his failure. This story, too, points up one lesson: Be faithful and obedient to the task assigned until the Lord returns.

In Matthew 25:1–13 Jesus told the story of ten virgins and a wedding. Five of the virgins who were to be attendants at the wedding had oil for their lamps and were ready for the festivities; five of the virgins did not have extra oil. When suddenly there came the cry, "Behold the bridegroom; come out to meet him," all the virgins arose. The five who were prepared were permitted to go into the joy of the marriage supper; the five who were not prepared were shut out. Again Jesus closed the simple story with the admonition, "Watch."

In Matthew 25:14–30 Jesus told the story about a man who made a journey into another country. He gave responsibilities to his servants by giving to them certain amounts of money to invest for him while he was away. To one he gave five units of money; to another, two; to another, one. The amounts were given to each one according to his ability. Immediately upon the departure of the master, the servant who had received five units went out to invest the money. The one who had received two did the same. The servant who had received one unit simply buried his money in the earth. When the master returned, he called for a reckoning. The two wise servants came bringing to him the increase of goods due to their work. He commended them as good and faithful servants and gave to them additional responsibilities in intimate association with him. The servant who had hidden his money in the earth came making his excuses for not having used the money. The master rebuked him as a bad and lazy servant. He took from him the responsibility which had been trusted to him, gave it to another, and pronounced sentence of punishment upon the bad servant. This story has one important lesson: Be faithful at the task assigned and ready for whatever task the Lord will give when he returns.

The final story in this series of illustrations is the much-used story of the division of the sheep and the goats (Matt. 25: 31–46). Full interpretation of this story will be given in chapter 5. Here, however, it must be seen as a climax to all that Jesus has said relative to his second coming. When the Son of man comes, he will divide men as a shepherd divides the animals that are before him, putting the sheep on one hand and the goats on the other. In one group the Son of man, who is spoken of as the King, will put those who have indicated the genuineness of their relationship to him by their merciful attitude to others. Upon that group he will pronounce the blessings of the Father. In another group he will put those who by their unmerciful attitude to others have shown that they were not Christ's people. Upon them he will pronounce sentence of judgment, and they will go away from that judgment unto eternal punishment. The righteous will go away from it unto eternal life. It is a story which speaks of proper preparation for the inevitable hour of judgment.

So the question which the disciples asked was answered by Jesus, but not in the way they expected. They asked when the destruction of Jerusalem would be and what would be the sign of his coming as though in their minds all that would be one event. Jesus answered by saying that the destruction of Jerusalem was one thing; his second coming was another. No one can know just when his coming is to be. His coming is definite; when he comes it will mean blessing to those who are his and punishment for those who are not his. In relation to all of this there rings once again Jesus' statement, "What I say to you, I say to all—watch!"

In the light of all that Jesus taught regarding the time of his coming it appears clear that he would have it understood that his coming will be in a sense *unexpected*. This idea is reflected in Luke 12:39–40, one of the earliest statements of Jesus on the subject. A man's house was robbed. Jesus said that if the man had known when the thief was coming, he would have been watching for him. He followed the very brief story with a word of admonition, saying, "Be you therefore prepared, for the Son of man will come at an hour when you are not thinking." The emphasis appears to be on the unexpectedness of the coming of the Son of man. This same emphasis has been observed in the series of parables which Jesus used in the Olivet discourse. The parable in Mark 13:35 and Matthew 24:43 is that of the master of a house and appears to be the same story.

After the same pattern, the parable of the faithful and the wicked servant of Matthew 24:45–51 underscores the idea of the unexpected return of the Master. This was particularly true on the part of the wicked servant who said to himself, "My Lord delays his coming" (v. 48). In similar fashion the parable of the ten virgins (Matt. 25:1–13) points up the unexpected nature of the Lord's return.

The idea of the Lord's coming unexpectedly is also found in 2 Peter 3:10. Many Christians had given up all hope of the Lord's return and were scoffing at the idea. Peter gave assurance that the Lord will come and that he will come "as a thief in the night." This certainly does not indicate any silent and hidden event. In fact, the passage speaks of the heavens' passing away with a great noise and the earth's melting with fire. Rather, the expression "as a thief" points up the unexpected nature of the Lord's return; when men are giving no consideration to the fact of his coming, suddenly he comes.

Paul in 1 Thessalonians 5:1–3 emphasized this same idea and used the same illustration. He also pointed out that when men are saying "peace and safety," destruction falls upon them as suddenly as travail comes upon an expectant woman.

One of the most dramatic passages on this idea is from the teaching of Jesus and has to do with his illustration of the days of Noah and the days of Lot. On another occasion Jesus had used a part of this illustration with reference to the destruction of Jerusalem (Matt. 24:16–18). In Luke 17:22–37 he appears to use the same material in relationship to his return. The people in the days of Noah were so involved in the everyday things of life that they were leaving the consideration of God and God's judgment completely out of their planning. The practices mentioned here—eating, drinking, and marrying—were not specified by Jesus as being evil in themselves. The evil lay in the fact that life was carried on without consideration of God and his requirements.

Jesus also said that in the days of Lot men were eating, drinking, buying, selling, planting, and building; suddenly God's judgment came in fire and brimstone from heaven. Again the emphasis does not appear to be on the excessive wickedness in the days of Lot, though that is well known. The emphasis is rather on man's being so preoccupied with the everyday life of this world that he does not give due consideration to God and impending judgment. Jesus said that his coming will be like that. It will mean the division of men into two groups, as sharply as two men working in the same field or two women grinding at the same mill are divided one from the other. It was this very unexpected nature of his return that caused Jesus over and over to underscore the imperative, "Watch!"

In connection with the unexpectedness of the Lord's return, the New Testament gives emphasis to the *imminence* of the Lord's return. A transition point from the idea of unexpectedness to the idea of imminence is observed in 1 Thessalonians 5:1–8. There Paul spoke of the unexpectedness of the Lord's return as far as the world in general was concerned. Christians, however, knew that the Lord will come as a thief in the night and were supposed to be prepared for and watching for his coming. They were not to be like the people of the world; they were to be alert, living the kind of life that will not cause shame when the Lord shall return.

This idea of the imminence of the Lord's return has been emphasized since his ascension. It must be observed, however, that the idea of the imminence of the second coming is rejected by some interpreters of the Scripture and greatly qualified by others.

One of those who rejects the idea of imminence is Carroll, whose works have been cited previously. Carroll was pronounced in his acceptance of postmillennial eschatology. In brief, his view was that the world will become Christian through the transforming power of the gospel as it is accepted when presented through Christian preaching. When the world has experienced a thousand years of this blessed reign of Christian life and principles, Christ will return—hence the term postmillennial, the return of Christ after such a thousand-year period.

Several ideas entered into his view. He held that there can be no reign of true Christianity (that is, no millennium) until the Roman Catholic Church has been annihilated.[18] He held, too, that there can be no millennium until the Jews as a nation have been converted to Christianity.[19] All of this he understood would come through the power of the gospel. It is evident

---

[18] B. H. Carroll, "The Book of Revelation," *An Interpretation of the English Bible* (New York: Fleming H. Revell Co., 1913), p. 66.

[19] *Ibid.*

that there is no place in that interpretation of eschatology for the idea of the imminence of the Lord's return. Carroll made it very clear that he wanted his students to get the idea of imminence out of their thinking.[20] His scriptural evidence for ruling out the imminence of the Lord's return is a statement from Matthew 25:19. Jesus told a story to illustrate his coming —a story of a master who took a journey into a far country and left his servants with certain responsibilities. In verse 19 Jesus made the statement, "After a long time the Lord of those servants comes and reckons with them." Carroll emphasizes the expression "after a long time" to prove that Jesus meant from the very beginning that as far as men were concerned, his second coming would be a long time away. The only idea of imminence possible would be imminence from the viewpoint of God, that is, "a thousand years are as a day."[21] While some have shared this interpretation of Carroll, it has not been generally accepted.

Some interpreters have held to the idea of the imminence of the Lord's return but in a qualified sense. Such men as Scofield, Larkin, and Talbot speak of watching for the Lord, but they do not have in mind the second coming of Christ in the generally accepted sense, but rather what is called the "rapture" or the secret coming of Christ to take his church out of the world before the seven-year period of the great tribulation. Talbot[22] may be looking for the "rapture" at any time, since he says that he is looking and waiting for the door of heaven to open and the voice to call him to heaven.

Scofield and Larkin's position, however, is not one which will permit looking for the Lord's return at any moment even in the sense of the "rapture" which they discuss. Scofield's edition of the Bible and his correspondence course make clear

[20] *Ibid.,* p. 303.
[21] *Ibid.,* p. 305.
[22] Louis T. Talbot, *The Revelation of Jesus Christ* (Grand Rapids: Wm. B. Eerdmans Publishing Co., 1953), p. 68.

the view that this coming of Christ to receive the church could not be a reality until other broad prophecies had been fulfilled, such as the close of the church age, and the return of the Jews to re-establish their nation, rebuild their Temple, and re-establish Temple worship. Other prophecies, such as the restoration of the ancient Roman Empire and its coming to world dominance as the country over which the antichrist would rule, must be fulfilled before even this "rapture" coming of Christ could be imminent.[23]

Larkin [24] says pointedly that this knowledge was withheld from the early church in order to keep them in the attitude of watching for the Lord's return. If they knew that his return was not to come for several hundred years, they would not be watching for him. He is in general agreement with Scofield, except that he anticipates the antichrist to rule over a restored Babylon and not over a restored Rome. For these men the idea of the imminence of the Lord's return is certainly a qualified one.

Still another approach to the idea of the imminence of the Lord's coming in a qualified sense is that set out by Ladd.[25] His entire thesis is that there is no scriptural basis for dividing the second coming of Christ into two parts, "rapture" and "revelation," with seven years between the two events. The argument which he presents at that particular point is convincing and rather devastating. He holds, however, that while there is a possibility of the Lord's return in any generation, it cannot be anticipated at any moment.

Ladd holds to the view that the New Testament predicts a period of seven years of tribulation, which will be followed

---

[23] C. I. Scofield (ed.), *The Scofield Reference Bible* (New York: Oxford University Press, 1945), pp. 1330–34; *The Scofield Bible Correspondence Course* (Chicago: Moody Bible Institute, 1907), II, 329–55.

[24] Larkin, *op. cit.*, p. 18.

[25] George Eldon Ladd, *The Blessed Hope* (Grand Rapids: Wm. B. Eerdmans Publishing Co., 1956), pp. 89–167.

by the Lord's return. It is apparent, then, that the return of the Lord cannot be expected until the end of such a period; one would have to determine when that period starts before he could anticipate the Lord's coming at its end. He holds that conditions could develop very rapidly and that it could be within this generation, but it could not be just at any moment; it would have to be several years away at the very minimum.

Another reason that he holds this view is related to his position on the task of the church, which is to spread the gospel of Christ throughout the entire world. The gospel has been preached to most of the world. Ladd holds that any generation which is really dedicated to the task can complete the mission of preaching the gospel to the world. This, he believes, is necessary before the Lord can return.

The main reason, perhaps, that Ladd opposes the idea of imminence is revealed in his interpretation of the New Testament imperative to watch. He holds that this does not mean to look for an event; rather, it relates to spiritual and moral wakefulness or readiness on the part of the Lord's people for his return whenever it is to be. He feels that the imperative "watch" was given because of the element of *uncertainty* as to the time of the Lord's return rather than because of its *imminence*.

Two objections may be raised to his position. One is that although the major emphasis in the idea of watchfulness relates to preparedness or readiness for the Lord's return, it is difficult to feel that the element of imminence can be entirely removed from many of the New Testament passages. Another objection is that Ladd too often associates the Lord's coming at any moment with a secret coming to "rapture" the church. In his insistence that the New Testament does not teach the latter, he practically eliminates the former. Many interpreters hold that the Lord's coming may be at any moment, but they reject the idea of a secret "rapture" of the

127

church. Their view is that the Lord may come at any moment, and when he does come, he will raise the dead, exercise final judgment, terminate the present world order, and introduce the eternal order. One can hold to the idea of the imminence of the Lord's return without holding to the idea of the "rapture" of the church.

It will be profitable to review representative New Testament passages in which the idea of the imminence of the Lord's return is reflected. A starting point may well be the Gospel parables on watchfulness recorded in Matthew 24–25. The parable of the talents, the parable of the faithful servant, the parable of the wicked servant, the parable of the master of the house, the parable of the ten virgins—all of these, while underscoring the element of preparedness or readiness, leave a rather overwhelming impression of imminence as well. In Peter's second sermon (Acts 3:12–26) the hearers were urged to repent, looking to the blotting out of their sins and to the return of Christ. In the light of the closing days of the Lord's presence with the disciples and his ascension, it is difficult to remove the hope of the imminence of the Lord's return from this passage.

In James 5:8–9, recognized as one of the very earliest Christian writings, encouragement is extended to the recipients of the letter: they should be patient unto the coming of the Lord and should establish their hearts, because his coming was near and the Judge already had taken his stand at the door. Similarly, in Hebrews 10:25 the readers were encouraged in the matter of assembling for worship, particularly in the light of the fact that "you see the day approaching." This, too, appears to be a reflection of the hope of the imminent return of the Lord. In the same chapter the believers were encouraged in the area of Christian patience and endurance by the statement, "Yet a little while and he who comes will come and will not tarry" (v. 37).

In 1 Peter 4:7 there is the idea of the expected consummation of God's purpose in the statement, "The end of all things
is at hand, therefore be you sober and watch unto prayer."
Paul reflected the same idea in Philippians 4:5 in the statement, "The Lord is at hand." Perhaps Paul's emphasis on
imminence is found, too, in his use of the pronoun "we" in
1 Thessalonians 4:17 and 1 Corinthians 15:52 when he spoke
of those who would be living when the Lord returned. It is
easy, of course, to say that this was no more than the use of
the editorial "we" according to modern habits of speaking or
writing. This refutation is not entirely convincing, however,
in the light of Paul's hope for the Lord's return and the life
beyond.

It appears that the idea of imminence of the Lord's return
was so emphatic in the minds of many believers in the New
Testament that some fell into serious error in their application
of the teaching. That appears to be the difficulty mentioned in
Paul's second letter to the Thessalonians (2:1–12). Paul related
the discussion in this chapter to his statement in 1 Thessalonians 4:13–17 regarding the coming of the Lord and the
resurrection. He had seemed by using the pronoun "we" to
put himself in the class of those who would be living at the
Lord's return. He had insisted, too, upon preparation and
watchfulness in the light of the imminence of the Lord's return
(1 Thess. 5:2–8).

It appears that some of the Thessalonians were disturbed,
understanding either from that epistle (or, as some hold, from
a forged epistle) or by some claim of a special revelation that
the Lord's coming was so immediately imminent that they
had given up work and were making of themselves busybodies
and troublemakers in the Christian fellowship (2 Thess. 2:2;
3:6–12). It was necessary for Paul to explain that he did not
mean to emphasize the imminence of the Lord's return in such
a way as to lead the Thessalonians to such folly. He explained

that the Lord's return would be preceded by other events —the falling away, the revealing of the man of sin, and the removal of the restraining one. What is meant by these things has long been a subject of controversy.

The first one, the falling away, is not particularly difficult. Jesus himself had spoken of times of turmoil which would be faced by his followers. By the time this epistle was written many Christians, facing persecution, had turned from their profession of being a part of the Christian movement. Other such periods were inevitable. Paul knew that the cause of Christ was destined to suffer great reversal, in which professed believers would betray it and forsake it on a vast scale. Some such desertion or repudiation is involved here.

The second development which would have to take place before the Lord's return was the revealing of the man of sin. The Greek expression "son of" is a very strong descriptive term, speaking of one's nature, of one's distinguishing characteristic. This man of sin was the son of perdition or destruction. He is described in 2:4 as one who opposed all that is called God; he exalted himself in opposition to all that is called God, even setting himself up as an object of worship. This one was destined to be revealed (that is, unveiled or uncovered) in his own season (v. 6). This one (also called "the mystery of lawlessness") was already at work (v. 7). Paul spoke in verse 5 of the fact that he had discussed these matters with the Thessalonians when he was present with them. Again in verse 8 he emphasized that this lawless one or son of perdition was destined to be destroyed by the triumphant Christ when he should return.

Interpreters have been greatly divided over the identity of this man of sin. Is he to be a man? There was no one in Paul's day who seems to answer the description given here, and this one was already working then (vv. 5, 7). Some of the language in this passage seems to indicate that the man of

130

sin is a principle rather than a person. "Mystery of lawlessness" is a neuter noun in contrast to the masculine "the lawless one" in verse 8 and "son of perdition" in verse 3, so the case cannot be settled on the basis of the gender of the term used.

The characteristics of this man or principle are clear. It opposes the God of Christian revelation and exalts itself to a place of worship (v. 4). It claims supernatural power, but the power proves to be false power from Satan (v. 9). It is recognized as the highest enemy of Christ (v. 8). The Thessalonian Christians knew what Paul was talking about because he had discussed these things with them while he was at Thessalonica. Full knowledge of his teaching there would make clear what he has in mind here.

In connection with this man of sin, or lawless one, there is also "the one who restrains." The word "now" (v. 6) may mean "accordingly" or "this being the case." If it does, Paul was saying to the Thessalonians, "You remember that when I was with you I told you these things, and this being the case, you understand the one who restrains to the end that this man of sin may be revealed in his own time." This mystery of lawlessness was already working, but there is one who restrains until the restrainer shall be taken out of the way. Then the lawless one will be revealed or uncovered, and the Lord will destroy him by the breath of his mouth and the brightness of his coming.

Who or what was this one who was restraining? This force was working in Paul's own day since his readers recognized its operation (v. 6). It was already restraining and would continue to do so until the proper time for the revealing or uncovering of the man of sin; then the restraint would be stopped (v. 7). Clearly it was some operation which was holding in check that which was opposing and seeking to destroy the Christian religion. Paul recognized that such restraint would not always be exercised. He knew that when that restraint was lifted and the "man of sin" was seen in his true nature (v. 9), he would be destroyed by the coming of the Lord. If there is to be detailed fulfilment of this passage, God has buried the mystery of it in his future purpose.

It may be profitable to observe different interpretations which have been suggested in efforts to identify the man of sin and the one who restrains. These are some of those interpretations:

The Man of Sin	The One Who Restrains
1. The man of sin was Jewish persecution in opposition to Christianity. This diabolical (more than human) operation was already at work. It was destined to continue until God's own time for stopping it.	1. The one who restrains was the Roman government, which held the Jews in check. When the day came that this restraint was stopped, the Jews would be seen in their true color and destroyed in judgment.
2. The man of sin is the Roman Catholic Church. Already "false" Christianity was beginning to develop. It would continue until "the Church" became completely apostate. The view is congenial to the postmillennial interpretation of Revelation.	2. The one who restrains is the existing moral or legal order, which keeps the Roman Catholic Church in check and prevents its exercising its full purpose. Its destruction is inevitable.
3. The man of sin was a coming personal antichrist who would make himself a rival to Christ for man's worship and devotion. The "principle" already at work in Paul's day was destined to become a "person" in the end-time. This view is congenial to premillennial eschatology.	3. The one who restrains is the government which will hold the antichrist in check and oppose his coming to full power. When that restraint is removed, however, the antichrist will be seen in his true nature and destroyed by Christ at his coming.

4. The man of sin is Satan himself. He was working in Paul's day and was destined to grow in power until "in his own season" his true character would be unveiled, and he would be destroyed by Christ at his coming.

4. The one who restrains is the Holy Spirit. He keeps Satan from exercising his full power. One day he will release that restraint and Satan will be seen in his true character. Then Christ will come and destroy him.

The major objection to the fourth view is that the language is very lofty to express so simple an idea. The points in favor of the idea are many: (1) Satan was already at work. (2) He was destined to increase in power. (3) He was inevitably doomed to failure and ruin. (4) The climax of his defeat is to be in connection with the Lord's second coming. (5) This view is consistent with the remainder of the New Testament. Views 1 and 4 do not conform to any particular system of eschatology.

One other matter related to the time of the second coming must be observed. That is the emphasis in the later writings of the New Testament on the fact that the *last stages of God's redemptive movement will be characterized by evil and hypocrisy.* In writing to Timothy about his work in establishing and strengthening the churches and giving instruction to church officers, Paul said that in later times some would fall away from the faith and give attention to false doctrine, led by hypocritical men who spoke lies and whose consciences were seared over as if burned by a hot iron. Some of these false teachings appear to relate to those of the gnostics. Paul charged Timothy to be alert for such opposition, to keep himself in good spiritual condition, and to warn Christian leaders against these false teachings.

In 2 Timothy 3:1–9 Paul spoke again of the grievous times to come in the last days. Men will become lovers of self and of material gain; they will be haughty and boastful in spirit, disobedient to parents, unthankful in their outlook on life, and unholy; they will be given completely to a life of pleasure. Such people, Paul said, would hold to a form of godliness but would deny the power of that godliness. Timothy was to turn away from them. They were of such evil character that they would draw those who followed them into a life of impurity. Timothy was to withstand them as Moses withstood the false religious leaders of Pharaoh.

Such men were destined to defeat. Their evil works could go so far and no further, as Jannes and Jambres were able to go only so far in their attempt to duplicate the miracles which were performed by Moses. Paul reminded Timothy of the difficulties which marked his Christian ministry and predicted that all who live the godly life in Christ Jesus will suffer opposition. Evil men and false religious leaders will continue their work of deception, but God's true representative has complete equipment, in the Scriptures, for his service in the world.

This idea of opposition to God's redemptive movement is reflected, too, in 1 John 2:18–29. John stated that his "little children" had reached "the last hour." Interpreters emphasize the fact that the Greek is without a definite article and can more properly be translated "it is a last-hour kind of time." As was true in the epistles to Timothy, so it is true in this epistle: this opposition to the redemptive work of God in Christ was already in operation. The writers felt that already the world had entered into the last stages of God's redemptive purpose; Satan already was doing his utmost to defeat the work of God.

In this passage John called attention to the rumor, which his readers had heard, that an antichrist was coming. Without commenting on that prospect he said that already many antichrists had arisen; by that sign these Christians could know that they were living in the last stages of God's redemptive purpose. These antichrists were those who had once professed to be a part of the Christian group. They had left that group and were denying that Jesus was the Messiah. It was John's view that the one who denied the sonship of Christ did not know the fatherhood of God, and the one who denied the fatherhood of God and the essential incarnation of God in Jesus was antichrist.

The Proper Attitude Toward His Coming

There is no area of the subject more important than this one. A study of church history and the history of the interpretation of the Scriptures reveals many instances when Christian fellowship has been disrupted because of wrong attitudes toward the doctrine of the second coming of Christ. There have been divisions in fellowship, distractions from major responsibilities in Christian service, and charges and countercharges as men have disputed the fine points of this doctrine. Here, as in so many other places, men agree on the matters of major importance; they disagree on the matters of minor importance.

From the viewpoint of practical Christian living, what does the New Testament have to say regarding the proper attitude toward the Lord's coming?

Preparation.—Many of the passages previously discussed in this treatment reflect the idea of preparedness. For instance, in Luke 12:40 Jesus concluded one of his stories with an exhortation to preparedness, "You keep on becoming prepared because in what hour you are not thinking the Son of man comes." This appears to be a rather abrupt translation, but it is an exact translation of the present imperative verb and the emphatic pronoun which Jesus used. Personal responsibility is found in the emphatic pronoun "you." Continuous action is involved in the present imperative of the verb meaning "to become," and this is followed by an adjective meaning "prepared"; hence the translation might also be "make a habit of

135

being prepared." Whatever one's view of the details of the Lord's coming, he should be prepared for it.

This idea is found in many of the parables which Jesus told: the master of the house (Matt. 24:43; Mark 13:35); the faithful and the evil servant (Matt. 24:45 ff.); the ten virgins (Matt. 25:1–13). These references are by no means exhaustive. They are only representative of the many passages in the teach- ings of Jesus and throughout the remainder of the New Testa- ment where an emphasis on preparedness is registered.

Expectation.—Expectation is naturally related to the former idea of preparedness, and yet there is a difference in emphasis. Doubtless there are many devout Christians today who are prepared for the Lord's coming who are not in the attitude of anticipation of his coming. In the New Testament there are many exhortations for the Lord's people to live in the attitude of anticipation of the Lord's return. In an earlier part of this work we have discussed the fact that the imperative "watch" cannot be related simply and only to the idea of being ready for the Lord's return. We have observed that doubtless that is a part of the emphasis, but it seems to be impossible to take from the imperative all of the temporal idea of watching. Jesus' emphasis was to this effect: because of the *certainty* of the *fact* of the Lord's return and because of the *uncertainty* of the *time* of his return, Christians should be alert in anticipa- tion of that experience.

All the New Testament passages regarding attitude toward the Lord's return imply the outlook of anticipation or expecta- tion. Representative of these, in addition to all which we have seen from Jesus himself, are 1 Thessalonians 5:6–8 in which Paul said that believers are not to sleep as unbelievers but rather they are to be watchful and levelheaded as they antici- pate the Lord's return, Titus 2:13 where Paul spoke of looking for the glorious experience of the Lord's return, and Philippians 3:20–21 where Paul spoke of our waiting for the return of the

Lord from heaven to bring to us the experience of resurrection. Nowhere in the New Testament does the idea of waiting involve the element of idleness. In 2 Thessalonians Paul rebuked those who were so captivated by the idea of the imminence of the Lord's return that they had quit working while they waited for his return. They were living off the brethren and causing trouble. Neither does the imperative "watch" mean that we are to keep our eyes turned to the clouds of heaven to catch the first glimpse of the Lord's return. Such interpretation misses the spirit of the imperatives relative to watching and waiting. They involve the idea of anticipation, but it is anticipation which marks those who are busy doing the Lord's work as he gave commandment.

Patience.—No characteristic is more becoming the Christian than the characteristic of patience. Patience, however, must be understood in its New Testament significance rather than in modern usage. In the New Testament there is no element of the folding of the arms and the easy chair in the use of the word "patience." Two words in two separate passages may illustrate this. One is Hebrews 10:36–37: "You constantly have need of patience in order that when you have done the will of God you may inherit the promise, for yet a little time the one who comes will come and will not delay." The word here translated "patience" is ὑπομονή. This noun form is derived from the verb μένω meaning "to abide" and the preposition ὑπό meaning "under"; hence, "to remain under." It speaks of the ability to stay under the load when it is heavy. This appears often in the New Testament as a characteristic of the Christian as he faces up to the responsibility that is his. There is constant need of this quality of staying under in relationship to every Christian responsibility and, according to the present passage, this is specifically true relative to the Lord's return.

Another passage emphasizing a similar idea is James 5:7: "Therefore, brethren, be long suffering until the coming of the Lord." Here the Greek verb is μακροθυμέω. The word means "to bear long" without resorting to the unchristian conduct of retaliation or violent reaction. The grammatical construction is an aorist imperative which looks on the total life of the Christian as one act of bearing long until the Lord's return. Continuing the idea, James spoke of the man who tills the soil waiting for the rains which will make possible the harvest. Steadfast endurance as he looks to the end of his labor at harvest time marks him; steadfast endurance is to mark the Christian as he looks to the end of his labor and harvest time relative to the Lord's return. The Christian is not to become discouraged when the promise of the Lord's return is not realized. He is to do his work, that which is God's will for him, in the spirit of steadfast endurance as he looks to the end of his labor and the harvest of the fruit of his labor.

Joy.—We should rejoice because of the Lord's coming. In 1 Peter 4:12–13 this idea is found. Peter spoke of the difficulties that were being encountered by the Christians of his day. They were facing many fiery trials which served as a means of demonstrating the genuineness of their religion. Peter encouraged them in the midst of their difficulties and told them to rejoice in the fact that they were sharing with Christ in the matter of suffering because of their relationship to God and the redemptive program of God among men. He told them, too, that their rejoicing should extend beyond this life and its difficulties and should embrace the experience of the Lord's return. In relationship to the Lord's return he exhorted them to "rejoice with abounding joy." The thought of the Lord's return should be at all times an occasion of rejoicing for the Christian. He should rejoice because of what it means to him personally. More than that, however, he should rejoice because of what it means in the consummation of the purpose of God for all men. The Lord's return means ultimate triumph of the redemptive purposes of God, and that ultimate triumph can for the Christian mean only rejoicing.

Holy living.—One of the greatest needs of our day is that of genuine piety. Not an assumed, artificial, or superficial piety, but genuine goodness which the living Christ would produce in men. This genuine devotion and godly living should mark the Christian for many reasons. One of the reasons given in the New Testament is that of the Lord's return. While this is found at many places in the New Testament, it is most pointedly expressed in some of Peter's writing. For instance, in 1 Peter 4:7–11 Peter urged the Christians in the light of the imminence of the Lord's return to be "of sound mind." This means to recognize the proper values. It means to be able to put supreme value upon that which is of supreme value and to make secondary or even more unimportant those things which are secondary or unimportant. What greater need has Christianity today than the need of people who have a proper sense of values, who know the value of things eternal in contrast to that of things temporal? In this same passage Peter urged his readers to be "sober with reference to prayer." This speaks of seriousness in one's prayer life. Jesus said that prayer was like a child talking to his father about the things he needs (Matt. 7:7–11). If that is the case, how very important it is that we should be serious in our prayer life, in our communion with God. While it is an experience that is open to all of God's people, it is an experience that is not to be regarded as common. It is an experience which is always to be recognized as a lofty privilege and a matter of the greatest importance. Again in this same passage Peter exhorted the Christians to be above everything else "fervent in love" among themselves. They were to be warm in their love one for another. When warm ties of love bind people together, there will be an absence of dividing influences at all points of doctrine and practice.

In verses 10 and 11 Peter urged the Christians to use the spiritual gifts which were theirs through the sovereignty of God. Whatever gift or ability one has he is to use in his service to God, and not the least motivation for that useful service is the motivation of the realization of the Lord's return.

This idea of holy living in relationship to the hope of the Lord's return is further expressed in 2 Peter 3:14. There Peter stated that since we look for an end to this world order and the beginning of the eternal order in relationship to the Lord's return, we should be diligent to the intent that we be found "without spot and without blame in his sight." The word translated "diligence" is one which conveys the idea of direct and energetic activity. Far back in the usage of the verb it meant literally "to jump fences." While one would hardly translate it in that way in a formal translation of the New Testament, that force makes it very meaningful. So it was, according to this word, that the shepherds in response to the angelic announcement of the birth of Jesus went to Bethlehem "jumping fences" ("they went with diligence," Luke 2:16). They did not look for the superhighway. They went directly across the fields to find the One who was born Saviour of the world. In the same way we are to take direct and energetic action to see that our lives are without spot and blemish in order that when the Lord returns there shall be no element of embarrassment or shame on our part and no element of reluctance in greeting him.

Peace with the brethren.—In this same passage (2 Peter 3:14) Christians are enjoined to be at peace with one another. This simple statement should be sufficient to cause the Lord's people to refrain from strife and bitterness over the doctrine of the Lord's return or any other matter that we hold in common. Whatever view one holds of the Lord's return, it should be of such nature that it encourages him to live in peaceful relationship to his fellow man. There is nothing within the

140

doctrine itself to cause men to divide into camps and take up weapons or words to battle over the subject. There can be disagreement without unpleasantness. There can be difference of opinion within the bounds of Christian fellowship. During the years of World War II it came to be very popular to say, "I love peace enough to fight for it." However worthy that profession in other areas, it should be recognized as an unworthy attitude where matters of division over secondary questions relative to basic Christian doctrine are concerned. Personally, I number among my warm personal friends men of every "millennial" approach to eschatology. None of us are mad about our differences, and we can join heartily in singing "Blest Be the Tie."

Evangelism.—We should be diligent in evangelism in view of the Lord's return. This appears to be what Peter had in mind when he said in 2 Peter 3:15 that we should look upon the delay of the Lord's return as a matter of salvation. His long-suffering with men and the delay of his return means an opportunity for witnessing to the truth of Salvation which is available through his redemptive work. We do not know when he shall return. We can be busily engaged in witnessing for him until he shall return. That witnessing will have the blessings of God in the bringing of still others to know Christ as Saviour and Lord. This diligence in witnessing is not limited to any particular approach to the Lord's return. Men of every and no "millennial" approach to eschatology have engaged and do now engage in witnessing to sinful men regarding the salvation which God has made possible through Christ.

Loyalty to God's truth.—We should be loyal to the truth of God. The hope of the Lord's return and the consummation of God's purpose among men is an incentive to loyalty to the truth. Such is the case presented in 2 Peter 3:17. There a warning is given that believers not be carried away by the error of wicked men. The particular point of reference may be error at the point of denying the Lord's return due to the apparent delay of the fulfilment of his promise. This, however, is only a probability. It may be that the entire body of revealed truth is what Peter has in mind when he cautions against being carried away by error. This would be in accord with Paul's statement to Timothy when he charges him to be loyal in keeping the commandments of God without spot and without reproach until the appearing of our Lord Jesus Christ (1 Tim. 6:14–15). This command follows immediately Paul's discussion of anyone who would not give assent to the teachings of Christ and to the doctrine which is related to godliness. Such persons are inevitably destined to judgment. A part of their mischief is that of leading others astray from the true faith. In contrast to that Timothy is to fight the good fight of faith and be true to the commandment which God has given. All of this is given by Paul as a charge related to the truth of the Lord's return.

Growth in grace.—We should grow in grace. The entire paragraph of 2 Peter 3:14–18 is one of the finest expressions of the practical side of the doctrine of the second coming to be found anywhere in the New Testament. The closing part of the statement is a very positive assertion in verse 18 that in the light of the Lord's return Christians should grow in the grace and knowledge of Christ. The Christian life is never a static one. By means of the spiritual birth the Christian begins his pilgrimage as a babe in Christ. Ideally, however, he is not to remain a babe in Christ. The normal experience is that of growth and development toward maturity as a child of God. In this statement Peter uses the doctrine of the second coming of Christ as an incentive to spiritual growth and maturity. The more one grows in divine favor and in his knowledge of Christ and the way of life which Christ would have his people to follow, the more he approaches that element of spiritual maturity which should characterize the children of God.

Doing God's work.—Turning again to some of the parables which Jesus used in his teaching relative to the second coming, we observe the emphasis which he made at the point of our being busy at whatever task the Master has given. This is found in the parable of the talents (Matt. 25:14–30), in the parable of the faithful servant (Matt. 24:45 ff.), and the parable of the master of the house (Matt. 24:43; Mark 13:34–36). Most implicit in this is the suggestion that we be busy at the task assigned. The corresponding suggestion is that such activity will be preparing us for whatever task the Lord shall have for us when he returns. One of the most encouraging statements relative to our eternal destiny is that found in Revelation 22:3 in the last description of our eternal home. The statement is "his servants will serve him." We do not know what kind of work God will have for his people through eternity, but we can know that whatever it is we shall do it with rejoicing and we are to do his work here in this world in the same spirit. One cannot think of heaven as a life of eternal idleness. Surely it will be a life of praise and service to our Redeemer. So the proper attitude toward the Lord's coming is an attitude of being busy at the task he has given us here and an attitude of getting ready for whatever task he shall give us for eternity.

The Consummation of the World Order

The total scope of the consummation of the world order and the beginning of the eternal order cannot be presented at this point; it must wait for the discussion on judgment and eternal destiny. It is important, however, that brief note be made here of the relationship of the second coming of Christ to the consummation of the world order. According to the New Testament the second coming of Christ will bring about the resurrection of the dead. This was observed in 1 Thessalonians 4:16 and 1 Corinthians 15:23, 52; it seems to be implied in 2

Thessalonians 1:8–10. It has also been observed that the second coming will bring about the transformation of the living so that they can never die (1 Cor. 15:52). The second coming will also end the separation of the Lord and his people (1 Thess. 4:17). All of this surely speaks partially of the consummation of the world order and the beginning of the eternal order.

While the major discussion remains for the next chapter, there is a definite connection between the second coming and final judgment. In Luke 17:34–36 Jesus indicated that his coming would mean a separation of the righteous from the wicked, as sharp a separation as division between two people working at the mill, one of whom would be taken and the other left. In Matthew 25:31–46 in the story of the division of the sheep and the goats Jesus spoke of judgment. Verse 31 definitely relates this judgment to the second coming: "When the Son of man shall come in his glory, and all the angels with him . . ."

In closing the story Jesus said that the wicked would go away from that scene unto eternal punishment and the righteous unto eternal life (v. 46). This appears specifically to relate the second coming to the consummation of this world and the beginning of the eternal one. In other places the same idea is underscored. The coming means judgment of the wicked and exaltation of the redeemed (Matt. 19:28). Christ at his coming will judge the living and the dead (2 Tim. 4:1) and will destroy the man of sin (2 Thess. 2:8). These are only representative passages of the many which relate the idea of the second coming to that of the consummation of the world order.

At other places in the New Testament brief and suggestive statements are made relative to the second coming of Christ and the eternal order. These statements are suggestive and thought-provoking, but they are never explained fully, and this lack of explanation has led to much conjecture on the part of interpreters. For example, Peter said (Acts 3:21) that Jesus is in heaven until the time of the restoration of all things. He said no more than that. All that is involved in this restoration (ἀποκατάστασις) is not indicated. Does it refer to the material world itself, or does it refer only to God's relationship and purpose for men?

Another suggestion Peter made is in 2 Peter 3:10–13. In the day of the Lord's return, Peter said, the heavens will pass away with a great noise. The earth and all in it will be burned as the elements melt in fervent heat. Already he had said that as the ancient world perished by means of the flood (v. 6) this present one was stored up for fire (v. 7). Continuing in this same vein in verse 12, he spoke of the heavens' dissolving in fire and the elements' melting with fervent heat. It may be that the word translated "elements" has reference to the heavenly bodies, i.e., the stars, etc. If this is the case, Peter indicated the dissolution of the universe as man knows it now. In place of that which is destroyed in this fashion, Peter said that there will be new heavens and a new earth in which righteousness will dwell (v. 13). The word translated "new" in each instance is καινός, "new in kind." There will be a new kind of heaven and earth, one marked by righteousness.

There is only enough in this passage to provoke thought and conjecture. It is clear that these events have to do with the end of the world order and the introduction of an eternal one in relationship to Christ's second coming. It is the divine purpose that the present order shall not stand forever. There is to be a complete change. Whether or not the things mentioned here are to be literal is not known. It is extremely doubtful if this passage should be made the basis for any cosmological program for the end of time.

According to the New Testament, the Lord's coming is certain but the time is uncertain. His coming will be mysterious but self-evident. No one will need to be told that it has become reality. His coming will mean the resurrection of the dead and the transformation of the living, final judgment upon men, and the close of the temporal order and the introduction of the eternal order. His coming places responsibility upon men to be prepared, to be watchful, to live at peace one with another, and to be faithful to the task assigned.

5.

Judgment

GOD'S final judgment of men is assumed in the New Testament. Scripture passages in abundance support this assumption. Most of these passages are presented not to prove the fact of judgment but to warn men of its coming. Certain words stand out as descriptive terms wherever judgment is mentioned: separation, blessing, punishment. There are many illustrations of judgment in the New Testament. There are, however, three basic pictures or concepts which have led to division of opinion on the subject: the sheep and goat judgment (Matt. 25:31–46); the judgment seat of Christ (Rom. 14:10; 2 Cor. 5:10); and the great white throne judgment (Rev. 20:11–15).

Do these speak of three separate judgments or are they different ways of looking at one judgment to come at the end of the world? Some [1] hold that these are different judgments, taking place at different times, for different purposes, and with reference to different people. The sheep and goat judgment will take place on earth and is God's judgment upon the *nations* to determine which nations shall continue in the

[1] C. I. Scofield (ed.), *The Scofield Reference Bible, in loco;* Clarence Larkin, *The Book of Revelation* (Philadelphia: Rev. Clarence Larkin Estate, 1919), pp. 178 ff.; and others.

world during the millennium. The judgment seat of Christ takes place in heaven during the seven years of the great tribulation on the earth and is a judgment on *believers*. While this judgment is taking place in heaven, the Jews are being judged by the great tribulation on earth. The great white throne judgment takes place in the air while the earth is being purged by fire at the end of the millennium and is judgment upon the *wicked* of all the ages.

This distinction of judgments was not recognized in New Testament interpretation until the middle of the nineteenth century and the work of John Nelson Darby, the founder of the Plymouth Brethren Movement. The system was expanded and published as a part of the Scofield Reference Bible at the beginning of the twentieth century. The Scofield Bible, more than any other one thing, has popularized the view and has caused many to accept the system as a part of the Bible itself. The view has *not* been accepted by the major groups within the Christian faith.

An exegesis of the three passages in question is a necessary preliminary to the discussion of the general subject of judgment.

The Sheep and Goat Judgment
(Matt. 25:31–46)

The setting of this story is important and instructive. It is the last illustration that Jesus used in answering the question of the disciples about the destruction of Jerusalem, the second coming of Christ, and the end of the world. It must be recalled that in answering their question Jesus divided the subject into two parts. He first discussed the destruction of Jerusalem; then he discussed the second coming and the end of the world, indicating clearly that the two were separate events. Concluding his discussion of the second coming, he used a series of stories to recommend preparedness, watchfulness, and faithfulness. This story, told with beauty and solemnity, closed that discourse spoken only three days before Jesus' death.

In the parable Jesus spoke of the Son of man as a King who, occupying a throne of glory and accompanied by all his angels, exercises the solemn task of judgment by way of separation of the righteous from the wicked. The expression in verse 32, "Before him will be assembled all the nations," indicates the universality of the company. What a solemn and impressive company it is—Christ the King, all his ministering angels, and all of humanity before him! His picture of separating men as a shepherd separates the sheep from the goats was a figure well known to his hearers. A shepherd would often separate a mixed flock into two groups for more effective feeding in the pastures. Such separation, too, was often done at night.

The separation that takes place in this account is a separation of men. The expression "all the nations" is used to indicate the universal nature of the company; it must be noted, however, that when the separation takes place, the pronoun that is used is masculine ("he will separate *them* one from another") and refers to people of the nations.

Those who are reckoned as sheep are put on the right hand of the King, a place of honor. He addresses them as blessed and as those who are inheriting the kingdom made ready for them from the foundation of the world. They are on his right, blessed of his Father and heirs of the kingdom because of their relationship to him, a relationship reflected by the attitude of compassion, mercy, and helpfulness which they have shown to others. Jesus expressed their ministry in terms of hunger, thirst, destitution, sickness, and imprisonment.

These "righteous ones," those who are right with God, are surprised at Jesus' statement that they have fed him when he was hungry, have given him drink when he was thirsty, have clothed him when he was improperly clothed, and visited him when he was sick. The emphatic position of the pronoun indicates something of this: "Lord, when did we see *you* hungry . . . When did we see *you* a stranger . . . When did we see *you* sick?" All that these people have done by way of merciful ministry was only the natural outreach of love and compassion which was theirs because they were identified with Christ. The King's answer indicates that such was the case, "Truly I say to you, whatever you have done to one of these my brethren, even these least ones, to me you have done" (v. 40).

The King will then address those on his left. He commands that they shall go away from him into the eternal fire which was prepared for the devil and his angels. Every clause and phrase in his statement increases the terror and the drama. "Go away from me" is within itself sentence of doom. The best reading of the text has no article for the participle "cursed." Without the article it is qualitative and speaks of the character of those addressed. "Into the fire," too, is an expression of terror, and that terror is magnified by the addition of the adjective "eternal." The terror is climaxed by the statement "which is prepared for the devil and his angels." This eternal fire, prepared for the devil and his evil angels, comes to be the fate of men who choose the devil and his way rather than Christ and his way. They will indeed reap what they sow.

The same terms which were used concerning the righteous are used in a negative fashion to indicate the failure of the wicked: "I was hungry and you gave me no food; I was thirsty and you gave me no drink." These, too, shall respond in amazement. Their answer will be that they never saw him hungry or thirsty or a stranger or improperly clothed or sick or imprisoned. Their failure has been a negative one. They have not seen others as the proper object of compassion. Their

150

failure at that point reflects their lack of recognition of Christ and a proper relationship to him.

Failure to exercise compassionate ministry on those who are Christ's and in need is failure to give proper recognition and attention to Christ himself. The essence of the entire passage is that the ultimate test of relationship to Christ is the test of life and of love. Those who are his recognize that and give themselves to such ministry, not as those who seek merit but as those who would express the love which is in their hearts. On the other hand, those who do not know Christ fail at the point of sympathetic ministry to those who are in need.

Jesus' closing statement is one that is filled with both glory and doom. These wicked ones go away from that judgment scene "into punishment eternal." The righteous ones go away "into life eternal." The two words that point up the ultimate result of judgment are the words "punishment" and "life." The word that is translated "punishment" is one which bears the idea of penal affliction and suffering for wrong done. The word which is translated "life" is the word which means life on the very highest plane. It is the life which one comes to possess when he comes to know Christ, and it is never lost to him. The same adjective is used to describe both. It is "punishment unending," just as it is "life unending." Full discussion of this concept is reserved for the chapter on eternal destiny. It is necessary to note here, however, that there is eternal life for the righteous and eternal punishment for the wicked.

A few questions briefly answered may summarize the meaning of this passage: (1) When does this judgment take place? It takes place "when the Son of man comes in his glory." Throughout the New Testament that means at the second coming of Christ. (2) Who is judged in this judgment? This is the judgment of all. The comprehensive nature is observed in the fact that all the nations are there. God is not just a God who rules over the Jews. He is one to whom all are responsible and before whom all will be judged. Those who are judged are judged as individuals (not as nations) as the masculine pronoun indicates and as the sentence pronounced upon them indicates. (3) What is the basis for the sentence pronounced? The basis is the genuineness of one's relationship to Christ, and that is reflected in the life which he has lived. All the New Testament doctrine of salvation by grace through faith in Christ is embraced in the term "the righteous ones" which is used for those who are blessed by Christ. (4) What is the outcome of this judgment? For the righteous it is the receiving of the heritage which is theirs as children of God—life eternal. For the wicked it is the very opposite. There is no heritage for them. There is only the sentence of doom: "Go from me, cursed, into the fire eternal which is prepared for the devil and his angels . . . And these shall go away into eternal punishment." The closing statement of Jesus should make it clear that he was dealing with judgment on individuals and not nations. Nothing is said about nations entering into any kind of kingdom; rather, it is the righteous ones who enter upon their rightful heritage with Christ.[2]

The Judgment Seat of Christ
(Rom. 14:10; 2 Cor. 5:10)

The Greek word which is translated "judgment seat" is βῆμα. This word and the two passages of Scripture indicated serve as a basis for the idea of some interpreters that the righteous are judged at a different time and place from the wicked. The entire concept is, as before stated, related to the idea of Christians' being taken out of the world while the wicked are left

[2] For further study of the passage according to this interpretation see the discussion in the previously cited works of Barnes, pp. 269–73; Broadus, pp. 507–15; Bruce, pp. 304–307; Ellicott, pp. 156–57; Lenski, pp. 986–1001; and in addition, Sherman E. Johnson, "The Gospel According to Matthew," *The Interpreter's Bible* (Nashville: Abingdon Press, 1951). These are representative of many who follow the same approach.

in the world for a period of time before the beginning of the millennium. During this time the Christians are spoken of as being sifted before the judgment seat of Christ in heaven. For some interpreters there is the parallel idea that while they are being sifted before the judgment seat of Christ in heaven, the Jews are being punished by the judgment of the great tribulation in the world.

The word $\beta\tilde{\eta}\mu\alpha$ itself must be investigated. It is used in the New Testament twelve times. In Matthew 27:19 and John 19: 13 it refers to Pilate's judgment seat at the trial of Jesus. In Acts 12:21 it refers to Herod's judgment seat; in Acts 18:12, 16–17, to Gallio's judgment seat; and in Acts 25:6, 10, 17, to Festus' judgment seat. In Acts 7:5 the word appears but is translated "a place." The reference is to Abraham and his original coming out of Haran into the land which ultimately would be given to his descendants but which was not given to him at that time, not even "a place of foot." This may mean that Abraham was not given at that time even a place big enough to stand on or it may have the sense of authority such as it has in other places, from the viewpoint that God did not give him a place there to exercise authority or rule. At any rate, it is clear that the general usage of the term simply means a place of the exercising of authority or judgment.

The first of the two places where the word is interpreted as a separate judgment on believers only is Romans 14:10–12. This is in the practical or ethical section of the Roman letter, in which Paul considered the way Christians should live in relationship to one another in a community, in the state, etc. The particular matter before him was that of the law of love in facing lines of conduct where differences of opinion may exist, such as eating a certain food or observing certain religious days. Paul's view was that the primary relationship is to God and not to others; he held, however, that in these relationships Christians must make room for loving consideration and not give themselves to judging the conduct of their fellow men. They were to leave the matter of judging to God, the righteous judge.

In this connection Paul wrote, "We will all stand before the judgment seat of God" (v. 10). He quoted Isaiah 45:23: "As I live, says the Lord, to me will bend every knee, and every tongue will confess to God." He followed the quotation with the statement that each person will give his own reckoning to God. The passage has been understood generally as referring simply to the matter of individual responsibility before God.

There is nothing in the passage that would speak within itself of any judgment other than the general judgment toward which all the New Testament points. Those who hold that this is a separate judgment call attention to the fact that Paul used the pronoun "we" in reference to Christians. That, of course, is true. He was talking about Christians, their relationship to one another, and their responsibility to God. There is nothing, however, to indicate anything other than a general reckoning with God which judgment promises for all men, Christians included.

The other passage which is used in this way is 2 Corinthians 5:10: "For it is necessary for all of us to appear before the judgment seat of Christ, in order that each one may receive back the things which he has done through the body, whether worthy or unworthy." The passage was fully discussed in the chapter on the resurrection. It reflects Paul's determination to be pleasing to God in every condition of life since one day he must appear before Christ in judgment. The Greek verb δεῖ involves a moral necessity in order that a desired end shall be realized. It is morally necessary that every individual appear before the judgment seat of Christ so that each one individually shall be recompensed for what his life has been. The passage speaks only of the certainty of judgment and the giving of rewards or punishment. There is nothing in the passage to

154

suggest anything other than the general concept of judgment which is found throughout the New Testament.[3]

The Great White Throne Judgment
(Rev. 20:11–15)

The last judgment scene which appears in the Bible is this one which speaks of sovereign and holy justice. The scene comes, in the book of Revelation, after all the affairs of men in this world have been worked out, after every effort of Satan and his evil forces has been defeated, and after Satan has been cast into the lake of fire with the allies who assisted him in his efforts to destroy Christianity. With that the earthly scene closes, and the curtain opens on the eternal. The idea of judgment is pictured by a king on his throne dispensing justice to all those who are before him. The terms used to describe the throne—great and white—speak of sovereignty and holiness. The fact, too, that all of creation recoiled from the presence of the One who was on the throne speaks of sovereign, holy justice. In his presence there is room only for that which is of eternal value.

In verse 12 John spoke of seeing those who were present for judgment. They were the dead, great and small, and they had taken their stand before the throne, ready for sentence to be pronounced. Again in verse 13 they were identified as those who had been in the clutches of death, and no matter what the condition of their death or burial, they were present here at the judgment bar of God. No one will escape that solemn and holy hour. Wherever men are, the long arm of God reaches them to bring them to a final accounting before him. All of the terminology here leaves the impression that all are present, not just some special class of people.

[3] For further study of the passage from this viewpoint see the previously cited works of Bernard, p. 68; Calvin, II, 225–26; Gould, p. 176; and Lenski, pp. 1014–17. Many others could be cited.

In the last part of verse 12 the basis and the method of judgment are pointed out. There are books there which include the record of the works of all who were present. There is another book, the book of life; this book of life is the roll of the Lord's people (v. 15). There is ample background for this concept elsewhere in the New Testament. When the seventy sent out by Jesus on a preaching mission returned to report to him their success even to the extent of casting out evil spirits, Jesus responded by saying, in part, "Rejoice not that evil spirits are subject to you; rejoice rather that your names are written in heaven" (Luke 10:20). The thing that brings greatest rejoicing to the believer is the realization that his name has been recorded in heaven as a part of God's people.

In Revelation 3:5 when the Lord was commending the faithful Christians at Sardis, he said that the ones who overcame would be arrayed in garments of white to indicate their victory; their names would not be blotted out of the book of life. In ancient days many cities kept a roll of the citizens of honor. The heavenly city also has a roll of honor, and it includes those who were the Lord's people. During the persecution under the Emperor Domitian in some centers rolls were made up of those who refused to worship the emperor because of their loyalty to Christ. One after another, as these people were brought to trial and punished, they were marked off the roll. The Lord encouraged his people by saying, "Your names may be marked off Domitian's roll, but they are not marked off the roll of the book of life." In Revelation 13:8 all men worshiped the beast except those whose names were in the Lamb's book of life. The book of life in this judgment scene speaks of the roll of the Lord's people.

It is understood, of course, that all of this is presented in striking symbol. Certainly no one would hold that it is necessary for the eternal God to write down the names of all his people or all the deeds of men so they will not be forgotten. This figure is merely a way of saying that a man's record will be complete and open when he comes to the hour of judgment. There he will be before a Judge who has all the evidence, a Judge of absolute justice and wisdom, who will know exactly the right sentence to pass in each particular case. This is not always the case in human courts.

How this judgment will be carried out is not discussed. The books might be used in something of a check and countercheck system. Here is a person who is to be judged. First, the book of life will be opened. If his name is written there, he will be identified as one of those who belong to the Lord, and the Lord's work in redemption will cover his sin. The Lord's perfect record will take the place of his imperfect record, and his eternal destiny will be with the Lord in the eternal home.

Another person stands before the judgment bar to be judged, and when the book of life is checked, it is clear that he is not included in that book. The only thing which he can plead is the record of his life in the book of deeds. That record will be insufficient, and according to the nature of his work and its inadequacy in the presence of a holy and just God, he will find his sentence to be one of doom, shut out of the holy city and consigned to the second death which is the lake of fire.

It is not necessary to think of every individual's standing while the two records are checked in order to find what his destiny is going to be. When the eternal and omniscient God is involved in the action, such activity is not necessary. People of sincere interest have sometimes been concerned over very minute problems relative to this scene of judgment. Questions have been asked even about the amount of time that would be necessary for such a judging of individuals. While this may reflect sincere interest and concern, it also reflects the finite mind of man and his inability to grasp eternal truths. However judgment is worked out, there will be no problem from the viewpoint of time, evidence, or sentence.

The outcome of this judgment is clear. Those who belong to the Lamb and whose names are in the Lamb's book of life go away from this judgment into the blessings of the eternal home which God has prepared for them. Those whose names are not in the Lamb's book of life and who have only their own sinful record to plead go away into eternal punishment.

In summary it may be observed again that the similarity of this scene to the sheep and goat judgment scene rules out any necessity of thinking of them as different judgments at different times for different people. All people are present here, as in the former scene. Judgment is on the basis of what one's total life has been, including his relationship or lack of relationship to Christ. The outcome of this judgment is the same as that of the sheep and goat judgment: For the righteous it is an eternal destiny of blessedness in the presence of the Lord; for the unrighteous it is a destiny of eternal punishment banished from the presence of the Lord.[4]

The Agent of Judgment

The idea of the agent of judgment may appear to be too elementary for inclusion in such a discussion as this. However, it is a basic part of the biblical concept of judgment. Granted a righteous God and a sinful man, judgment follows as a natural corollary. If God is righteous, he must exercise mercy on the obedient and mete out punishment to the disobedient. He would be as unrighteous if he left off judgment for the wicked as he would be if he left off blessings for the righteous.

When sinful man is placed in the picture, the truth is all the more evident. If man is a moral creature, he is a respon-

[4] For further study of the passage from this viewpoint see the previously cited works of Carroll, pp. 321–32; Lenski, pp. 599–612; McDowell, pp. 204–6; Summers, pp. 209–11; and many others.

sible creature. As a responsible creature he is under an obligation imposed by the righteousness of his Creator. To rebel and to engage in sin must call for punishment; to obey and to follow the way of God must call for blessings. One cannot posit a righteous God and an unrighteous man without moving into the area of responsibility and judgment.

In the New Testament a majority of the references to judgment speak of the eternal God as the agent. According to the teachings of Jesus, men are not to fear the wrath of those who have power to kill the bodies only; they are to fear the one who has the power to cast them into hell (Luke 12:5). Majority opinion understands this to have reference to God.

In this section of his teaching Jesus told his disciples to trust in the loving care of God, not that of irresponsible men; they were to fear the wrath of God, not the displeasure of men. God's wrath is upon the disobedient, those who do not receive the redemption which God has offered through his Son (John 3:36). The parable of the marriage feast which the king gave for his son pictures God as the king. It was the king who gave the order that the unprepared guests be bound hand and foot and cast into outer darkness (Matt. 22:1–14). This idea is repeated in Acts 17:31 in the statement that it is God who will judge men through and in relationship to Jesus Christ.

The general epistles continue this same emphasis. In James 5:1–6 God's judgment on the wicked is clearly stated. It is God who judges, and his judging is without partiality (1 Peter 1:17). It is God who judges, and his judgment is righteous (1 Peter 2:23). According to 1 Peter 4:5 the one who judges appears to be the eternal God; in 2 Peter 2:4–22 God is the agent of judgment. The Epistle to the Hebrews speaks in clear terms of God as the agent in judgment. According to Hebrews 10:30–31 vengeance belongs to God, and it is a fearful experience for the wicked to fall into the hands of the living God. In Hebrews 12:23 God is pictured as the just judge. These references to God as judge, particularly as they reflect the idea of the kind of judge involved, are one with the concept of God as judge to be found in Hebrew thinking in the Old Testament and in the intertestamental literature.

Paul, too, spoke of God as the agent in judgment. God is the avenger of evil (1 Thess. 4:6); his righteous judgment will be pronounced upon wicked men (2 Thess. 1:5). It is a righteous thing for God to repay anguish to those who are persecuting his people (2 Thess. 1:6). The wrath of God is an indication of judgment. The wrath of God (his constant fixed displeasure against evil) is a matter of divine revelation (Rom. 1:18), just as his righteousness is (v. 17). The wrath of God is upon the Hebrews who, in their rejection of Jesus Christ, have rejected his message and method of salvation (Rom. 9:22). Vengeance belongs to God and is not to be exercised by men (Rom. 12:19). Everyone individually will give a reckoning unto God for what his life has been (Rom. 14:10–12).

In many other passages, particularly in the Gospels, Christ is spoken of as the agent of judgment. His first coming established the principle of his judgment. This is reflected in the statement in John 9:39: "For judgment I came." It is reflected in the statement made by John the Baptist concerning the One who was coming after him: "His winnowing fan is in his hand and he will thoroughly cleanse the threshing floor" (Matt. 3:11–12; Luke 3:15–17).

The principle of Christ as the agent of judgment established at his first coming continues to the end and the consummation of God's purpose. In the day of final judgment it is Christ who will say to those who make false profession to be his, "Go away from me; I never knew you" (Matt. 7:23). It is the Son of man who will send his angels at the end of the world to gather the tares for burning and to gather the grain into everlasting granaries (Matt. 13:41). It is Christ who will sit on his throne and judge men (Matt. 19:28; Luke 22:30). This Stone rejected by the builders will fall with crushing judgment upon those who have rejected him (Matt. 21:44).

Judgment and the authority to execute judgment are given to the Son (John 5:22, 27). The judgment which the Son exercises is righteous judgment (v. 30). In the parable of the sheep and goats it is the Son who sits as a king on his glorious throne and makes the division of those who are before him (Matt. 25:31). It is Christ who will judge the quick and the dead (Acts 10:42; 2 Tim. 4:1). Christ's coming into the world meant separation of the good from the bad; when the final day of separation and judgment shall come, the eternal Christ will carry out that work of division.

One other suggestion must be treated. That has to do with the idea that Christians, too, shall have some part in judging. There are a few passages in the New Testament which no more than hint at this role of Christians. These passages have sometimes been joined with others to make more of the idea than appears on the surface. In Matthew 19:28 Jesus told Peter that the apostles would sit upon twelve thrones and judge the twelve tribes of Israel when the Son of man sat on the throne of his glory. This statement was part of Jesus' answer to Peter's question about what the disciples were to receive in return for having given up everything to follow Jesus.

A similar statement was made by Jesus on the night before his death on the cross (Luke 22:28-30). The apostles who had stayed with Jesus through his many trials were told that he was appointing unto them a kingdom; they would sit on thrones judging the twelve tribes of Israel. Some interpreters [5] understand this to teach that when the Lord returns, he will set up an earthly kingdom with headquarters in Jerusalem and will rule through the twelve apostles over the Jewish people

[5] See Scofield, Larkin, Talbot *in loco*.

restored to Palestine and through his followers, the Christians, throughout the rest of the world. This is a very large and elaborate system to be based on so brief and uncertain a statement. Other interpreters [6] understand that this judging on the part of the twelve apostles relates only to the example of their testimony. That is, when the day of judgment comes, their testimony concerning the truth of the gospel will condemn the people who rejected it. The reference may be to the power of their testimony against unbelieving Israel. This is a possible and reasonable interpretation of the statement; it is more in line with the remainder of the New Testament on the matter of judgment.

In 1 Corinthians 6:2–3 Paul sounded a note similar to this statement of Jesus. The setting is his rebuke of the Christians at Corinth for their inability to settle difficulties between themselves. They were going before pagan judges with lawsuits to settle their difficulties. The contradiction in their position is obvious. Here were people who were supposed to live by the controlling power of love, which was not known by the pagan world. So far were they from the ideal, however, that they were going before pagan judges to settle difficulties among themselves. Paul rebuked them and encouraged them to settle their difficulties either by having a fellow Christian act as a court of arbitration or by suffering loss in the matter rather than going before a heathen court and bringing a bad name to the church.

A part of Paul's encouragement was in his statement, "You know, don't you, that the saints will judge the world?" and "You know, don't you, that we will judge angels?" This is a very brief statement to be used as any part of a system of judgment. It is most likely that Paul had in mind the teach-

---

[6] George R. Bliss, "Commentary on the Gospel of Luke," *An American Commentary on the New Testament* (Philadelphia: American Baptist Publication Society, 1881).

ing of Jesus just discussed. At that time the teachings of Jesus made up that oral gospel which was precious to the Christians and which they used to determine doctrine and practice. Whether or not Paul had in mind Jesus' statement, there is no reason for believing that he meant any more than that which Jesus meant in suggesting that the witness of believers in accepting Christ and his lordship would one day be a means of judgment against the wicked men and rebellious angels who refused that lordship.

Revelation 2:26–27 is used, too, to point to a time when believers will share actively with Christ in judgment. This passage is a part of the Lord's message to the church at Thyatira. To those who overcame, Jesus said that he would give power over the nations; they would rule with him as he ruled, with a shepherd's staff of iron. Before them men would be broken as pottery vessels are smashed. Certain triumph was ahead for them just as certain triumph was ahead for him. Nothing in any of these passages promises actual ruling or judging on the part of Christians. By their loyalty to Christ they bring the witness which will be the basis of condemning those who have refused Christ. When all has been considered, the truth remains that God-in-Christ is the world's Redeemer, and God-in-Christ is the world's Judge. He and he only is the Judge.

The Time of Judgment

In the appendices of this book appear some comparative studies of several different ideas of the time of judgment. If one holds to the view of multiple judgments, the subject of the time of judgment is a very complicated one. If, however, one holds to the view of one general judgment, New Testament terminology is simple even though various emphases are indicated. This last view seems to be the better one.

Sometimes in the New Testament the time of judgment is

mentioned merely as a matter of divine appointment, as in Acts 17:31, where the assurance is given that "God has appointed a day" when he will judge men. Hebrews 9:27 has been used with the same emphasis, though the application is somewhat questionable. It appears that all that the writer was saying was that death is the appointed destiny for every man, but that does not end his experience; beyond death there waits judgment.

In Romans 2:5 reference is made to "the day of wrath," and in Romans 2:16 to "that day when God judges." These phrases refer merely to a day of judgment that is out in the future. They do not relate that judgment to any particular event. In similar usage (2 Tim. 1:12, 18) the expression "that day" is used with apparent reference to the time of judgment. Verse 12 contains Paul's assurance as he looked to that day and all that he had committed unto the Lord against that day. Verse 18 voices Paul's confidence that Onesiphorus, who had shown mercy to Paul the prisoner, would himself receive mercy at the hands of the Lord "in that day."

The same term is used in 2 Timothy 4:7–8; Paul spoke of having finished successfully the work which the Lord had given him to do. He was looking forward to the award which was to be given to him by the righteous judge "at that day." The award is not for Paul alone; it is for all who love his appearing. These are terms that speak of a time of judgment, but they do not relate that to any particular event.

There are also those passages which say that the time of judgment will be at the resurrection. In Matthew 12:41–42 and Luke 11:29–32 Jesus spoke of the men of Nineveh and the queen of the south who would be raised up in judgment against the wicked people of Jesus' own day. The verb that is used in the case of the men of Nineveh is the verb from which the noun "resurrection" comes. Literally translated, the passage would read, "The men of Nineveh will be resurrected in judgment with this generation and will condemn it." This would appear to connect the idea of judgment directly to the resurrection. There are other passages where this connection is the logical inference, such as those cited in Paul's writings in 2 Timothy 1:12–18 and 2 Timothy 4:8. It may be, too, that this idea is present in John 5:29; in this verse Jesus spoke of those who would experience the resurrection of judgment. The word "judgment" appears to include the idea of condemnation in contrast to the life kind of resurrection to be experienced by others.

The major emphasis in the New Testament on the time of judgment is that it will be at the second coming. The assurance that God knows how to keep wicked ones under punishment until the day of judgment (2 Peter 3:7) and the assurance following that the day of the Lord will come (2 Peter 3:10) suggest that judgment is related to the second coming of Christ. Judgment (1 Thess. 5:3) and vengeance upon those who do not know God (2 Thess. 1:8) are related to the second coming.

Paul stated in 2 Timothy 4:1 that Christ will judge the living and the dead at his appearing (which can mean only his second coming), and according to 2 Timothy 4:8 the crown of righteousness which Paul expected to receive "at that day" will be given at the second coming. All of this has its background in Jesus' own teaching.

It has been observed in passages previously considered that the idea of judgment is related to the day of the Lord's return in very definite ways. The coming of the Son of man means separation of the good from the bad—a separation that would take one who was grinding at the mill and leave the other (Matt. 24:40–42; Luke 17:34–36). The reference apparently is to a separation between two members of a single household working together at a millstone. The second coming of Christ means judgment that is of such specific nature that it will separate even two sisters or a mother and a daughter if one is rightly related to the redemptive program of God in Christ and the other is not. Judgment at the second coming is found, too, in Luke 19:11–27, the parable of the pounds; in Matthew 25:14–30, the parable of the talents; and in Matthew 25:31–46, the parable of the sheep and goats. All in all, it appears to be clear that the time of the Lord's second coming will be a time of judgment upon men in the consummation of God's purpose. Christ came once as Saviour and gave himself for man's redemption. He will come again to judge men on the basis of their acceptance or rejection of that redemption.

Another very specific idea relative to the time of judgment is that it will be at the end of the world. Two very meaningful parables of Jesus relative to judgment have not been discussed in detail. They are parables in which Jesus spoke specifically about judgment and the end of the world—the parable of the tares (Matt. 13:24–30; 36–43) and the parable of the nets (Matt. 13:47–50). In explaining the parable of the tares to his disciples, Jesus said specifically, "The harvest is the end of the world" (v. 39). He indicated that at that time there would be a division of the wheat from the tares, the righteous from the wicked, the children of the kingdom from the children of the wicked one (v. 38). Those who were the children of the wicked one would be cast into a burning furnace where there would be wailing and gnashing of teeth. Those who were the children of the kingdom would shine like the sun.

The same idea is in the parable of the nets. A few of Jesus' hearers would certainly appreciate this parable since they were themselves fishermen. Jesus pictured a net cast into the sea; it enclosed every kind of sea life. When it was brought to shore, however, the fishermen divided the catch, keeping the good and disposing of the bad. Thus, Jesus said, will it be "at the end of the world" (v. 49). The angels will sever

166

the unrighteous from the righteous and cast the unrighteous into the furnace of fire. Here again judgment is the theme which is underscored, and it is judgment at the end of the world. It appears, then, that all of the New Testament sees man and his world moving inevitably toward that great day which will mean the return of the Lord, the resurrection of the dead, and the final judgment upon men. That day will mean the end of this world order and the beginning of the eternal one.

The Objects of Judgment

The previous discussion points the way to treatment of the theme of the objects of judgment. All men will ultimately be judged of God. This would seem to be obvious. Brief treatment, however, appears to be in order due to the question so often raised as to whether or not all (or only the wicked) will be judged. The question may be asked in part because of a subconscious wish to escape the scrutiny of the all-seeing eye of God in judgment! The impression that is gained from the New Testament is that God's judgment is comprehensive where men are concerned.

According to Romans 3:19 it is clear that the whole world is accountable to God. This verse follows Paul's discussion of the evidence in the life of the Gentile and in the life of the Jew that both were under burden of sin and under sentence of judgment. Acts 17:31 gives the assurance that God will judge the world, and Jude 14–15 emphasizes the idea of the execution of judgment upon all. According to Romans 14:10–12 all men will give an account unto God, and according to Hebrews 12:23 God is the judge of all. It has been observed in the two major pictures of judgment (the sheep and goats and the great white throne) that the scope of judgment is comprehensive. All men are present in both. The righteous

167

leave the scene of judgment in blessedness with their Lord; the wicked leave under sentence of condemnation.

There are other statements in the New Testament which are of particular note as they seem to point to the comprehensive nature of judgment. In Acts 10:42, 2 Timothy 4:1, and 1 Peter 4:5 the indication is given that God will judge the living and the dead. This appears to mean all men, both righteous and unrighteous. Neither those who have died prior to the day of judgment nor those who are still living at the time of judgment will escape that day. All will give a reckoning. Those who think that only the wicked are to appear in judgment are frequently heard to say, "Don't look for me at the judgment; I will not be there!" That may be true. On the other hand, it seems that the New Testament view is that all men will be present for that ultimate judgment. Those who belong to Christ have nothing to fear. Christ's perfect record and atoning work cover their record. For them it will only be an experience which will vindicate the fact that they have been right in linking themselves to the redemptive program of God in Christ. For them the outcome can be only the pronunciation of the blessings of the Lord and the entrance into the eternal home with him. For those who have refused him and the offer of his love, however, the prospect can be one of fear; having spurned every offer of the love of God and having rejected the atonement that was offered to them, they have left themselves in the position of having only their own imperfect and inadequate records to plead for them at the bar of God's justice.

The Basis of Judgment

One idea which stands out throughout the New Testament where the concept of judgment is concerned is the fact that judgment—condemnation—will be related to one's total life or works. This has been observed in the three major pictures of judgment previously discussed: the sheep and goat judgment (Matt. 25:31–46), the judgment seat of Christ (2 Cor. 5:10), and the great white throne judgment (Rev. 20:11–15). In the sheep and goat judgment scene, while men were judged on the basis of works, it was a matter of works that indicated relationship to Christ. In the judgment seat of Christ passage, the statement was made that men will give an account unto God for all things done in the body, whether good or bad. In the great white throne judgment scene, those present were judged according to their works as these works were revealed in the books which were opened.

How specific the judgment on the basis of works will be is reflected in Jesus' statement, "I say to you that every idle word which men shall speak, they will give concerning it a reckoning on judgment day" (Matt. 12:36). The word translated "idle" is a word which means blameworthy. That is, every word which man speaks which by its nature is corrupt and worthy of blame will be a matter of reckoning with a righteous God in the day of judgment. In 1 Timothy 5:24–25 Paul stated that all sin is to be judged, whether hidden or open. There are some sins (or sins of some men) which are done openly. It is naturally assumed that such evil works will be judged. There are other sins (or sins of some men) which are kept under cover. These, too, will be judged in that day when the books are opened and when the record kept by the eternal God is manifest.

In 1 Peter 1:17 the observation is made that judgment will be on the basis of each man's works, and this is suggested as an incentive for every man to live out his life in the attitude of respect for God and the principles of judgment. Alexander, the coppersmith, will receive from the Lord in proportion to the evil work which he did in opposing Paul and his missionary work (2 Tim. 4:14). The wrongdoer will be paid back for the work which he has done (Col. 3:25). All of these references point up the matter of individual personal responsibility before God. A righteous God demands an accounting on the part of responsible men. The accounting will be in direct relationship to what the life has been.

In some passages in the New Testament references to works as a basis of judgment relate directly and specifically to sinful activity. In 2 Peter 2:6–9 reference is made to past judgments of God as an argument for a future judgment of God upon wicked men. If God in the past judged wicked angels (v. 4), wicked men in the day of Noah (v. 5), and the wicked cities of Sodom and Gomorrah (v. 6), he knows how to keep the unrighteous under punishment until the day of judgment. The judgments mentioned were judgments related to sinful conduct. The judgment promised in the future is also judgment related to sinful conduct. The same is true in Jude 12–15. There wicked men carousing together in evil living are mentioned as ones who are appointed for the dark blackness forever.

God's condemnation of all works of ungodliness is a certainty. In Luke 13:1–9 Jesus spoke of the certainty of judgment upon the wicked people of his day who refused to repent of their evil works and to bring forth fruit for God. Some questioners had called Jesus' attention to a tragedy that had occurred when Pilate had slaughtered certain Galileans in the act of worship. Their own blood had been mingled with the blood of the sacrifices which they were making. Jesus' questioners seemed to be asking, "Why did it happen to these Galileans and not to others? Was it because these were more wicked than others?" Here was the age-old problem of suffering and the quest for an answer to that suffering. Jesus' answer brought home to them their personal responsibility before God. First of all, he said no; that is, the reason for the death of these worshipers was not to be found in their excessive wickedness. His hearers waited breathlessly for him to give

170

the reason for this slaughter, but they were disappointed. Rather than giving the reason, he made a personal application, saying, "Unless you repent you will all perish like that."

At the same time Jesus used another illustration. A tower at Siloam had fallen, killing eighteen people. Naturally men would be raising the question, "Why were these killed? Was it because they were more wicked than others?" Again Jesus said that their wickedness was not the reason. Then he stressed personal responsibility by repeating, "Unless you repent you will all perish like that."

Jesus followed this alarming statement with a parable about a man who found that a certain fig tree in his vineyard was not bearing fruit. He suggested to his servant that since this tree had borne no fruit for three years it should be cut down. There was no reason for it to take up space in the vineyard unless it carried out its purpose in being there. The servant made a countersuggestion that the tree be left one more year. He would give attention to it by feeding it and digging around it. If after that additional opportunity it bore no fruit, then it should be cut down. Jesus probably had in mind here, as at other places, Israel as a nonbearing fruit tree. Israel had had many opportunities to carry out God's purpose for her in fruit bearing. Now she was having one more opportunity in relationship to the Messiah. Her failure at that point could mean only condemnation.

In some passages in the New Testament judgment or condemnation of men for their works is related very directly to their relationship one to another. In James 5:1-6 woes are promised to rich men; they have made themselves rich by oppressing and exploiting their fellow men. The riches which they have made will be testimony against them in the day of judgment. The payment which they have fraudulently withheld from the laborers in their fields cries out for justice. Thus to oppress and to exploit one's fellow men may bring wealth and position in this life, but such wickedness will be a basis of judgment upon men when they give their accounting unto God.

This concept of judgment on the basis of relationship to one's fellow man extends into the area of teachers and religious leaders. In 2 Peter 2 reference is made to false teachers who claim to be true representatives of God but who in reality deny the Master that bought them (v. 1). Peter may have had in mind his own denial of the Master in the long ago, an act which caused him an intense suffering of soul from which he was rescued by the Lord's appearance to him following the resurrection. These false teachers promise men much, but their promises prove to be empty. In verse 17 they are compared to springs without water and clouds without rain. For them there is only the judgment of God; there is reserved for them "the dark blackness."

In contrast to these false teachers, true religious leaders are commended in Hebrews 13:17. The readers of the letter are encouraged to obey their religious leaders, realizing that these leaders have a trusteeship from God and that they care for the spiritual interest of their followers as men who will give an account unto God for the way they have carried out their responsibility. These are leaders who have proved by their works that they are worthy of being followed, and on the basis of those works they shall give their account one day to God.

Paul may have had something like this in mind in 1 Corinthians 3:13–15. He compared a man's work in leadership for God to the building of a house. Jesus Christ is the foundation of that house. As the man builds the superstructure on that foundation, he makes a choice of material. One man chooses poor material for building the house, just as some men in Paul's day would build a house of wood or straw or even the stubble of the field ground up and made into a plaster-like material. Other men choose gold, silver, or marble. These materials are fireproof. Paul said that a day of testing will come when the works which each man has done will be tested by fire. If one has built his house of worthy and lasting materials, it will stand the test. If one has not built his house of such materials, he will find that all of his work will be swept away. Salvation is his, but he has suffered the loss of all that his efforts have built because he used the wrong materials in his building.

The commentaries [7] are in agreement that Paul's illustration here relates to work in the building of the church. To bring injury to a dwelling place of God is to incur his displeasure. Religious leaders will give an account unto God for the kind of work they have done in representing him and his cause. That judgment may sometimes begin in this life. Some men build a record of splitting churches to such extent that they can no longer be used in the role of leader. That within itself is partial judgment.

In connection with the idea of works as a basis of judgment, the New Testament speaks definitely of disobedience as a basis of condemnation. In John 3:36 Jesus spoke of the wrath of God upon one who obeys not.[8] In Luke 12:42–48 he spoke of the relative punishment of one who knew in comparison to one who did not know. The one who knew and disobeyed was worthy of more severe punishment than the one who was guilty of wrong but was not aware of its being wrong. Both were subject to punishment, but the one who was wilfully disobedient was subject to more severe punishment.

The followers of Jesus continued this emphasis on judgment for disobedience. In his sermon from the porch of the Tem-

[7] Representative of many who hold this view are Carroll, Findlay, Gould, Lenski, and David Smith.
[8] Some manuscripts read "believes not."

ple, Peter used Deuteronomy 18:19 as God's promise of judgment upon everyone who did not obey the prophet whom he would send. Peter understood that Jesus was the fulfilment of that promise, and he understood this passage to speak of God's judgment upon those who did not obey [9] Jesus (Acts 3:23). Attention has been given previously to Peter's view of God's judgment upon the rebellious angels (2 Peter 2:4). Peter thought that it was difficult for anyone to be saved (1 Peter 4:18). If this is true, what hope is there for the one who disobeys the good news of God and stands only in his own ungodliness and sin (v. 17)?

Jude spoke of wicked men who in their disobedience and rebellion did not hesitate to speak out against God's true representatives (v. 8). In contrast to their "railing at dignities," he said, Michael the archangel did not even bring a railing judgment against the devil when they disputed over the body of Moses. The picture presented is that of Michael and the devil's arriving concurrently to take possession of the body of Moses. Michael insisted that the body belonged to God, and the devil insisted that the body belonged to him. Even though the devil was an evil spiritual authority, Michael did not rail at him; he simply said, "The Lord rebuke you." These disobedient men, however, storm out against all spiritual authority wherever matters which they do not understand are concerned (v. 10). They have gone the disobedient way of Cain and Balaam. For them God's judgment and "the dark blackness" is reserved forever.

The author of the Epistle to the Hebrews spoke of the certainty of judgment for those who were going on in deliberate sin, even after they knew the truth: "If we go on sinning by deliberate choice after we have received the knowledge of truth, there is no more a sacrifice for sin but only certain fearful expectation of judgment and the fiery jealousy which will

[9] The verb is "hear," but obey seems to be the meaning.

174

devour the adversaries" (10:26–27). A person comes to know the truth of God's redemption provided in Christ. Knowing that truth, he deliberately turns his back upon it and goes on in his life of sin. This person has rejected the only available sacrifice and has left for himself the only alternative—God's judgment.

According to Paul, disobedience has a large place in God's judgment. This is stated nowhere in better fashion than in Romans 1:18 to 3:20. In this classic passage on man's condition in his sin Paul showed that all men were under sentence of God's wrath because of their own disobedience, the Gentile because he repudiated God's revelation through conscience and creation (vv. 18–21). In the place of the Creator he enthroned in his heart the sensual and material image of created things (vv. 22–23) and lapsed into the basest forms of impure living (vv. 24–27). When the Gentile chose to go this way rather than God's way, God let him go the way of his own choice. Because he made this choice, God's judgment is upon him.

In Romans 2:1 to 3:8 Paul looked into the life of the Jewish people and saw reflected there the same repudiation of God's revelation and hence the same sentence of judgment. While the Gentile had the unwritten revelation of God through conscience and the created order, the Jew had the written revelation of the Law. He refused to follow that written revelation and went the way of disobedience. Hence God's wrath is upon him.

Paul lined up many passages from the Old Testament to show the effect of sin in the life of all men, Gentile and Jew alike. Sin brings degradation of character (vv. 10–12), degradation of speech (vv. 13–14), degradation of conduct (vv. 15–17), and degradation of motive (v. 18). All men have disobeyed God's revelation; all men are under sentence of God's judgment.

Referring again specifically to the Jew, Paul made a very interesting play on words (10:16-21). All the Jews heard the way of God, but not all obeyed that way of God. The Greek word for "hear" is ἀκούω. The Greek word for "obey" is ὑπακούω. A transliteration into English will preserve the pun: "They all *akouoed* but they did not all *hupakouo!*" The same emphasis is presented in the English translation, though not so forcefully: "They all *heard* but they did not all *hearken.*" Because of this disobedience they were under judgment of God.

Another New Testament basis for judgment is unbelief. This, in the final analysis, is the supreme basis for condemnation. Wicked living, disobedience, and even rebellion are forgiven when man comes to make peace with God in Christ. Failure at this point, however, is the one supreme failure. Faith in the redemptive work of God in Christ is the one means of standing before God with security.

This view of unbelief as a reason for punishment has its basis in the teachings of Jesus. In Matthew 12:38-42 there is an account of Jesus' words to the scribes and Pharisees who came to him seeking for a sign. Apparently they wanted him to perform some miracle which would be so outstanding that, even apart from spiritual perception, they would be convinced that Jesus was God's representative. He denied them any such sign, indicating that the one supreme sign which would vindicate him as God's Messiah would be his resurrection. In connection with his illustration that he would be in the heart of the earth three days and nights as Jonah was in the belly of the fish three days and nights, Jesus commended the men of Nineveh for responding to the preaching of Jonah. He said that those men would be raised up in judgment against his own generation, which refused to repent at his preaching though he was greater than Jonah. In the same connection he said that the queen of the south would be raised up in judgment against his own generation because she showed great wisdom in coming to learn from Solomon while his generation was rejecting One greater than Solomon.

On another occasion Jesus spoke words of condemnation to the wicked Galilean cities which were rejecting him (Matt. 11:20–24). He had done mighty works in these cities. They, however, refused to turn from their error and exercise faith in him. He said that in the day of judgment the wicked Gentile cities of Tyre and Sidon would have an easier time than these Jewish cities. Likewise, he said that the wicked city of Sodom would have an easier time in judgment than New Testament Capernaum. That city was so hardened against Jesus that it would not exercise faith in him, while Sodom would have believed, even in all of its wickedness.

Similar judgments were registered by Jesus on other occasions. When he sent out the twelve on a preaching mission, he gave them instructions as to their conduct when they were rejected by any city into which they went. If their message was refused, they were to go on to another city; outside of the city which had rejected their message they were to stop and stamp their feet. (An Oriental messenger indicated in that way that his king's message had been rejected.) Jesus said that in the day of judgment the wicked cities of Sodom and Gomorrah would have an easier time than such a city as that. Such a city had sinned against much greater spiritual light and truth than any known in the days of Sodom and Gomorrah. Because of its unbelief it would be worthy of greater judgment. This teaching in Matthew 10:14–15 has a parallel in Luke 10:10–16 in the instructions which Jesus gave when he sent the seventy on a preaching mission.

The emphasis in all these passages is that of unbelief; condemnation is related to that unbelief. This idea is found, too, in Matthew 22:1–14. Those who spurn God's invitation are subject to judgment just as those who spurned the invitation to the marriage feast were blameworthy. The same idea

seems to be basic in the sheep and goat judgment passage of
Matthew 25:31–46. Basically it is the rejection of Jesus which
brings sentence of doom to one group and the acceptance of
Jesus which brings sentence of blessedness to the other. This
rejection or acceptance was reflected in the individuals' attitude toward Jesus' followers.

While unbelief as a basis of condemnation is found in the
Synoptics, it is the Fourth Gospel that is usually remembered
when this concept is mentioned. Unbelief in Jesus as the Christ
of God is one of the cardinal themes of this Gospel. One cannot
think of the Gospel of John without thinking of John 3:16 and
its statement of the love of God which sent his only begotten
Son into the world. The one who believes in the Son does not
come under God's judgment, but the one who does not exercise such faith is already under condemnation. The one who
exercises such faith has eternal life, but the one who refuses
to give obedience and faith to the Son has the wrath of God
abiding upon him (v. 36).

John 8:21–30 records Jesus' controversy with the Jews on one
occasion. He told them that he was going away and that they
would die in their sins unless they believed that he was all
that he claimed to be. There were those who believed in him
at that time, but the great mass of the Jews refused to believe
that he was the promised Messiah.

The entire ninth chapter of John, the fascinating story of
the healing of the man born blind, is a commentary on spiritual perception. This man, who experienced the miracle of
healing, came out of that experience to exercise faith in Jesus
and to worship him (v. 38). The Pharisees, who claimed to
have full spiritual perception, were so set against Jesus that
they would not accept him. They had even agreed that anyone who confessed Jesus to be the Christ would be put out
of the synagogue (v. 22). To these Pharisees Jesus explained
that if they were without spiritual perception, they would

not be guilty of the sin of unbelief. Their very claim to spiritual perception, however, joined to their rejection of him, meant that their sin was still upon them.

In his last public discourse recorded in the Gospel of John, Jesus made the statement that the person who rejected him and refused to receive his teachings would be judged by the word of truth which he had spoken; in the last day that word would judge the one who rejected Jesus (12:48).

This concept of unbelief in Christ as a basis for judgment is found throughout the First Epistle of John as well as in the Gospel. At no point is it better expressed than in 1 John 2:23. The one who denies the Son has not the Father, while the one who confesses the Son has the Father also. It is John's view that one cannot have the fatherhood of God if he denies the sonship of Christ.

Unbelief as a basis for judgment is an outstanding concept in the Epistle to the Hebrews. Ancient Israel failed to enter into the promise of God because they did not believe he could deliver to them the land that was inhabited by giants who lived in walled cities. Because they did not believe, they did not obey when he told them to go in and take the Promised Land (3:18–19). The author warned his readers that they should not be guilty of the same unbelieving disobedience which would cause them to fail to come into possession of what God held out for them.

Paul had his word to say about unbelief as a basis of condemnation. In the book of Romans this is particularly true. A classic example is that of the Jews, who were rejected of God because of their unbelief, while the Gentiles had come to be accepted of God because of their belief. In Romans 11: 11–24 Paul developed this idea. He pictured the Jews as a natural branch broken from an olive tree and the Gentiles as a wild branch grafted on. The Jews were broken off because of their unbelief; the Gentiles were grafted on because of their belief. At the time of Paul's writing these Gentiles were bearing fruit where Israel had failed. Paul warned the Gentiles, however, that if they did not continue to exercise such faith, they could be cut off from their fruit bearing for God, and he held out the hope that Israel would turn and exercise faith once more.

The last tragic word in the New Testament relative to unbelief as a basis for judgment is in Revelation 21:8. This verse is a dramatic contrast to verses 1–7, which describe John's vision of heaven as a tabernacle in which God is in intimate association and fellowship with his people. The old world has passed away and God on his throne says, "Look, I am making everything new!" (v. 5). Shut out of all of the glory of this scene are those listed in verse 8: the fearful, the abominable, murderers, fornicators, sorcerers, idolaters, liars, and the unbelieving. All of these have their part in the lake that burns with fire and brimstone. The words in this catalogue were used by the Christians in the day in which the book of Revelation was written to describe those who were outside the circle of the Christian religion. The word "unbelieving" might better be translated "faithless"; the faithless were those who had not exercised faith in the Lamb of God. To refuse to believe in him is to remain outside the circle of those who love him and who enjoy his fellowship for eternity. In the last analysis the supreme basis of God's condemnation of men is their relationship to Christ.

The Outcome of Judgment

It is fitting that the closing section of this chapter should deal with the outcome of God's judgment upon men. Preparatory to that discussion, however, the characteristics of God's judgment should be noted. Everywhere in the New Testament there is an emphasis upon the fact that God's judgment is righteous. In Romans 2:2; 3:6; 2 Thessalonians 1:5; and

2 Timothy 4:8 God is pictured as a just or righteous judge. In Acts 17:31 he is described as One who will judge in righteousness, and in 1 Peter 2:23 as a God who judges righteously.

God's judgment is also impartial. God is one that judges without partiality (1 Peter 1:17). Paul stated in Colossians 3:25 and in Romans 2:11 that there is no partiality with God; he is no respecter of persons. The term "respecter of persons" is a translation of a Greek word which is a compound of the verb meaning "to receive" and the noun meaning "the face." God does not receive anyone by facial appearance. This phrase echoes God's statement to his prophet of old that he does not see as men see; while men look on the outward appearance, God looks on the heart (1 Sam. 16:7). God judges according to the truth revealed in the gospel (1 Peter 4:5). Such true impartial righteous judgment is what men can expect when they come before God for their final reckoning.

In Hebrews 4:12–13 the term λόγος may not mean "word"; it may mean "reckoning." If this is the case, the writer is saying, in literal translation: "God's reckoning is living and energetic, sharper than any surgeon's knife, piercing even to the separating of soul and spirit, of joints and marrow, and adequately critical for discerning the hidden thoughts and purposes of the heart. There is no creature that is not clearly manifest in his sight, but all are exposed and laid open before the eyes of him, facing whom for us is the reckoning."

God is rigidly discriminating in his reckoning and completely discerning in his estimate of those whom he judges. The picture is that of the first-century surgeon's table. The patient is exposed in the bright light of God's wisdom. The discerning judgment of God is like the surgeon's knife to probe into the heart and lay bare its most secret thoughts and purposes. It is such a God and such a reckoning which man faces. How very solemn is that thought!

For the righteous the outcome of judgment is blessedness

with God. This has been reflected at many places in the discussion. In the parable of the tares, the parable of the net, the parable of the sheep, and the parable of the talents Jesus spoke of the blessedness of those who were his. In 2 Timothy 4:8 Paul voiced his assurance of the crown of righteousness which was to be his, and in 2 Timothy 1:18 he spoke of mercy and peace for God's people beyond judgment. In 1 Peter 5:4, having told the elders that they were not to serve out of a spirit of grasping for material gain, Peter said that their reward would be from the chief Shepherd. When the chief Shepherd comes, he will give to his servants a crown that will never wither or fade. In the next chapter, the eternal destiny of believers will be discussed. Here it is sufficient to observe that for the Lord's people the outcome of judgment means that blessed state.

For the unrighteous the outcome of judgment means the very opposite. For them it means a state of punishment such as that described in the parables that Jesus used. To the unrighteous the Shepherd-King will say, "Go away from me," and these will go away into eternal punishment. The concept of God's vengeance upon the unrighteous is reflected in 2 Thessalonians 1:8 and Romans 12:19. The concept of God's wrath on the unrighteous is emphasized in 1 Thessalonians 1:10; Colossians 3:6; Romans 1:18; and Romans 5:9. In Acts 3:23 ruin is the sentence of judgment upon the unrighteous. They shall be "utterly ruined." In Hebrews 10:27 there is the picture of the fury of fire which shall eat upon the adversaries. All of this, joined with the concept of being separated from the blessings and the fellowship of God (Heb. 4:3–4), paints a terrible picture of the fate of the unrighteous. Their ultimate state will also be discussed in the next chapter.

6.

Eternal Destiny

IN THE DAY of judgment a responsible creature will stand before his Creator to give an account of what he has done with the trusteeship of life. Beyond that experience lies mystery —mystery, that is, beyond what is given in God's revelation. Even that revelation is cast in the vocabulary of man and must be interpreted to the best of man's ability to understand it.

The first great problem is the question of the meaning of the word "eternal." In the New Testament this word is used to describe the destiny of both the righteous and the unrighteous. The classic example of this usage is Jesus' statement in Matthew 25:46: "And these shall go away into everlasting punishment: but the righteous into life eternal" (AV). The Greek text has one adjective which is translated in this passage in two ways, "everlasting" and "eternal." This translation is unfortunate and has led to unfortunate conclusions. The passage is better translated consistently: "And these will go away into eternal punishment, but the righteous into eternal life."

The bearing of this statement from Jesus on the duration of future punishment is a matter of tremendous importance. Although the question is too extensive to be determined by a single text, all that this text contributes to the answer must be fully weighed. If eternal life is to have no end, eternal punishment will also have no end. These are solemn words; Jesus meant for men to understand that the division between the righteous and the wicked in this judgment scene was one which will never be changed. Men must reap the result of their evil deeds as they will reap the result of their good deeds. In this sense they determine their own retribution, and so far as the New Testament speaks, without assignable limit. It is eternal punishment for one; it is eternal life for the other.

There has been such a tendency for man to understand eternal life as a new quality of life that the idea of duration is not considered. Hence men often express the view that eternal life refers not so much to *duration* of life as to the *transcendent nature* of life. The transcendent nature of the life of the believer is certainly to be granted as a New Testament concept. The one who comes by faith to be related to the living Christ experiences a quality of life which even in this world transcends his previous life, to say nothing of what his nature is to be beyond the limit of the physical. In granting this concept, however, the fact that the word αἰώνιος carried the idea of duration must not be left out. Jesus himself emphasized this idea when, speaking of one who possesses this new life, he used such terms as "he shall never die" and "he shall never perish." An investigation of the use of this adjective which is translated "eternal" is necessary and instructive.

Liddell and Scott [1] define the use of the word in classical Greek by the one word "perpetual." They go on to indicate that it is similar in usage to another Greek adjective, ἀΐδιος, which they define as meaning "everlasting" or "eternal." They would say, then, that in classical usage this word meant perpetual,

[1] Henry George Liddell and Robert Scott, *A Greek-English Lexicon*, seventh edition (New York: Harper and Brothers, 1883), p. 43.

everlasting, or eternal. The synonym ἀΐδιος is used only two times in the New Testament, in Romans 1:20, "his everlasting power and deity," and Jude 6, "angels . . . he has reserved in everlasting chains." In both these instances it appears that the adjective means "never-ending." That, too, appears to be the meaning of the more commonly used adjective αἰώνιος.

How was this adjective used in New Testament times outside of the New Testament? The most authentic answer to that question must come from Moulton and Milligan.[2] They review the use of this adjective in nonliterary and nonbiblical materials. Their conclusion is that in the vernacular, as in the classical Greek, αἰώνιος never loses the sense of *perpetuus. The Classical Latin Dictionary*[3] defines this word as "continuing, lasting, unbroken, uninterrupted, perpetual, forever."

According to Thayer,[4] this same force usually applies to the word's use in the New Testament. There is some variety of emphasis, but always there is present the concept of duration. In Romans 16:26 the word is used to describe God, who is without beginning or end. In Romans 16:25 it is used of time without beginning. In most instances in the New Testament, however, it refers not to that which is without beginning, or that which is without beginning or end, but rather to that which is without end, that which is never to cease, that which is everlasting. It is in this sense that it is used in such passages as 2 Peter 1:11; 2 Timothy 2:10; Hebrews 9:15; Hebrews 5:9; Luke 16:9, and in the multiplied instances when Jesus used the adjective to modify life.

The word is used in the same way to qualify the destiny of

[2] James Hope Moulton and George Milligan, *The Vocabulary of the Greek New Testament Illustrated from the Papyri and Other Non-literary Sources* (Grand Rapids: Wm. B. Eerdmans Publishing Co., 1949), p. 16.

[3] *The Classical Latin Dictionary* (New York: Hinds, Hayden and Eldredge, Inc., n.d.), p. 408.

[4] Joseph Henry Thayer, *A Greek-English Lexicon of the New Testament* (New York: American Book Company, 1889), p. 20.

the wicked in such passages as Hebrews 6:2; 2 Thessalonians 1:9; Matthew 25:41; Matthew 25:46, and many others.

Thayer [5] suggests that the adjective ἀΐδιος covers the complete philosophical concept of that which is without beginning or end, whereas the adjective αἰώνιος gives prominence to the idea of the immeasurableness of eternity. He suggests that this word is especially adaptable to usage with that which is supersensuous, such as life, death, truth, etc.

It appears that whatever qualitative sense is involved in the New Testament use of the word "eternal," the sense of duration is absolutely retained. Those who would reduce the punishment of the unrighteous to a shorter period must by the same token reduce the life of the righteous to a shorter period. It should, however, be noted that as Jesus used this word in Matthew 25:41, he used it in the scene of judgment which appears to be the end of the temporal order, so the word could not be understood in any limited sense. Lenski [6] raises the question that if this Greek adjective does not mean eternal, is there a Greek adjective that would carry that idea? If the word does not mean eternal, it is doubtful if there is a Greek adjective which would convey that thought, and in order to express it one would of necessity have to use a noun construction in a negative statement, such as "there will be no end."

There are, of course, those who recognize that "eternal" must be applied to punishment in the same way that it is applied to life. Representative of those who grant this but deny the sense of duration of "eternal" is Weatherhead. [7] He recognizes that whatever is said about the temporary nature of hell must be said, too, about the temporary nature of

[5] Ibid., p. 21.

[6] R. C. H. Lenski, *The Interpretation of St. Matthew's Gospel* (Columbus: Wartburg Press, 1943), p. 997.

[7] Leslie D. Weatherhead, *After Death* (Nashville: Abingdon-Cokesbury Press, 1936), pp. 66-91.

heaven. His view, then, is that neither heaven nor hell is eternal. He thinks of both as being temporary and preparatory for a new age in which there will be perfect life. All that has been called either hell or heaven will have passed away.

Weatherhead grants that this view is not consistent with the words of the New Testament. He feels that the only convincing argument in its favor is one based on the character of God. He thinks that hell is, by nature, remedial; it purifies for the ultimate state which lies beyond both heaven and hell. Therefore he states specifically that he does not believe that the soul's destiny is a settled matter at death; he does not believe that men are sentenced either to a final heaven or a final hell; and he does not believe that punishment is penal in nature.

Weatherhead is correct in at least one thing: his views cannot be based on Scripture passages. His view of God as one who would not hold man responsible for his sins for eternity leaves out much of the biblical insistence that because of his love God has done everything consistent with his righteous character to prevent men from spending eternity in punishment. In his righteous character, however, God must punish the disobedient as well as bless the obedient. According to this view, man chooses his own destiny when he chooses or rejects the love and mercy of God. Man is totally responsible for the destiny which he makes his own. If it is a destiny of punishment, it cannot be charged up to God as a matter of injustice on his part.

The Eternal Destiny of Unbelievers

Having surveyed the meaning of the word "eternal," which is used to characterize the experience of both the righteous and the unrighteous, we turn specifically to the question of New Testament teachings relative to the eternal destiny of unbelievers. Much of what is to be found here has already

187

been anticipated in the discussion in chapter 2 of the experience of the wicked immediately beyond death. The ideas presented here are descriptive of the eternal state of the wicked when the judgment of God has been carried out. The total impact of the life of the wicked man has been the basis for the sentence of judgment passed upon him.

Abode of the wicked.—What is to be said of the place or the abode of the wicked for eternity? This question is properly introduced in qualitative terms by the observation that for eternity the wicked are *separated from God.* How else can their destiny be expressed? We do well to remember that we are dealing with terms in an attempt to describe a condition that almost defies description. In Matthew 7:23; 25:41–46; and Luke 13:27 the command, "Depart from me," is given by Christ. Matthew 25:46 specifically indicates that the wicked will go away into eternal punishment. These terms "depart from me" and "go away" suggest separation from the blessings and fellowship of the Lord's presence.

These passages are not alone in presenting this idea. In Luke 16:25–26 the rich man in torment is told that there is a great and impassable gulf between him and Abraham. He is separated from the blessings that came to the beggar Lazarus in the bosom of Abraham. In 2 Thessalonians 1:9 Paul spoke of those who would experience exclusion from the presence of the Lord. According to Ephesians 5:5 evil men have no inheritance in God's kingdom. In the last picture given in the New Testament the unrighteous are shut out of the eternal city in which the righteous enjoy the immediate presence and fellowship of Christ (Rev. 21:8, 27 and 22:15). The doctrine of the omnipresence of God notwithstanding, to be shut off from blessings from him and fellowship with him is in point of fact to be separated from him.

The unrighteous have their eternal dwelling place in *hell.*

The English word "hell" is used to translate the Greek term γέεννα, which is a transliteration of the Hebrew term *Ge Hinnom*, that is, the valley of Hinnom or the valley of Lamentations. The valley of Hinnom was immediately southeast of the city of Jerusalem. In ancient times it had been the location of the worship of the heathen god Molech, which included burning babies alive. This practice was abolished by King Josiah (2 Kings 23:10), and the place came to be used by the Jewish people as a place for garbage disposal, including the refuse from the city, the bodies of animals, and even the bodies of criminals who had no one to give them burial. A fire was kept going continuously for sanitary purposes. The term "the Gehenna of fire" came to be a term very generally used to present the idea of that which is abominable.

In the New Testament this word is used in James 3:6 to refer to an undisciplined tongue, an instrument set on fire by hell. Other than that instance, the word was used only by Jesus. In Matthew 5:21–22 the term is found in Jesus' statement concerning guilt in connection with the commandment "You shall do no murder." Passing beyond the physical act of murder, Jesus said that one who holds the wrong attitude toward his fellow man is guilty of breaking this law; one who shows absolute contempt for his fellow man is punishable by the hell of fire.

The grammatical construction in this passage is one which was not used by classical Greek writers. The word ἔνοχος is used in connection with the preposition εἰς and the word for hell. Literally translated, Jesus' statement was that such a person "will be punishable in the hell of fire" or "will be liable to the extent of the hell of fire."

Jesus used the term two times more in this chapter. In Matthew 5:29 he spoke of the whole body as being "cast into hell" and in Matthew 5:30 of the whole body as "going" into hell.

Here, as in verse 22, he can have reference to nothing other than the place of punishment allotted the wicked.

In Matthew 10:28 and Luke 12:5 there are similar references. Jesus was giving advice to his disciples as he sent them on a preaching mission. He told them of the difficulties and danger which were ahead. He advised them to trust in the power of God to care for them and at the same time to fear the displeasure of God and not the displeasure of men. They were not to fear men who had power to kill the body but had no power over the soul. Rather, they were to "fear him who is able to destroy both soul and body in hell."

The setting of the passage in Luke is different but the emphasis is the same. Jesus warned his disciples against the hypocrisy of the Pharisees and told them of the evil days that were ahead of them. As in the Matthew passage, he said here, "Do not fear those who kill the body and beyond that have no more which they can do. Fear him who after he has killed has authority to cast into hell." God's displeasure is a thing to be shunned at all costs because his authority reaches beyond this life. He has power to consign men to hell for eternity.

In Matthew 18:9 and its parallel in Mark 9:43, 45, and 47 other references are made to hell. In Matthew 18:8 the "eternal fire" appears to have the same significance as the "hell of fire" in verse 9. Jesus was using the strongest possible language to warn men against a line of conduct which would lead to their being cast into the eternal fire, that is, into hell. The language of Mark 9:43–48 is most dramatic. Hell is described as a place of fire which does not cease to burn (v. 43). Each phrase adds force to the statement "to go away once for all into hell, into the fire which does not cease burning." The terror of the place is further described in verse 48 by the statement "where their worm does not die and the fire is not put out."

One other passage must be considered. In Matthew 23:15

Jesus pronounced woes upon the hypocritical scribes and Pharisees, who would compass both sea and land in an effort to make one proselyte. This proselyte, however, experiencing no inner spiritual change with his outward change, would bring into his new standing all his former evil and would add to that all of the evil of the scribes and Pharisees. Such a person, Jesus said, was made "twofold more a son of hell" than the Pharisees themselves. Apparently he meant that such a person was of such guilt that he deserved hell. In the same chapter (v. 33) Jesus condemned the scribes and Pharisees as the offspring of vipers and asked, "How will you escape the judgment of hell?"

A review of all these references will indicate that no one of them can possibly refer to the valley of Hinnom outside Jerusalem. In every instance Jesus was using the word which spoke to his contemporaries in terms of horror and abomination to describe the place of the eternal destiny of the wicked. This hell of fire, originally prepared for the devil and his angels as a place of punishment for their apostasy (Matt. 25:41), is to be the place of destiny for wicked men. In their rebellion against God and their rejection of his love and his mercy these men have turned to the devil and become like him. The devil and his angels, whose examples wicked men have followed on earth, are their companions in the eternal fire. These men themselves have chosen their place and their companions.

Experience of the wicked.—What is the nature of the unbeliever's life and experience? It is almost paradoxical that a question about the "life" and experience of the unbeliever in his eternal destiny is primarily answered in terms of death. Paul spoke of death as the wages of sin (Rom. 6:23). He said, too, that if one lives according to the flesh, he will die (Rom. 8:13). This does not refer to the physical experience of death, which ends life as it is known here. Rather, it has to do with the penalty of sin and the experience of the individual beyond the death of the physical body.

Paul spoke of sowing according to the flesh and reaping corruption, of sowing according to the Spirit and reaping life eternal (Gal. 6:7–9). Sowing seeds of disobedience in the field of the heart can result only in a harvest which Paul described as corruption relating to death. On the other hand, sowing seeds of obedience under the impulse of the Holy Spirit is to realize a harvest which is described by contrast in terms of life.

"Death" as a descriptive term for the destiny of the wicked is very graphically presented in Revelation 2:10–11 and 20:6, 14. In these passages the destiny of the wicked is termed "the second death." The believer comes to physical death and finds within himself a quality of life which does not end; it continues his sense of fellowship with God. The unbeliever comes to physical death and finds beyond it a separation from the blessings and fellowship of God which can be described only as a second death. This second death is further described in terms of fire.

The eternal destiny of the wicked is described in the New Testament as "destruction." Some passages from Paul are representative of this idea. In 2 Thessalonians 1:9 Paul spoke of those who will experience "eternal destruction from the face of the Lord and from the glory of his power." In the expression "from the face of the Lord" one sees again the concept of separation. To be cut off from the presence of the Lord means destruction or ruin. In Philippians 1:3–19 Paul affirmed that destruction is the end of the enemies of the cross. These, according to Paul, are people whose god is that which is sensual and whose minds are on things of the earth; in contrast, believers have their citizenship in heaven and think on eternal things. Paul experienced great distress as he considered the fact that there were such people, and he wept as he spoke of those who were enemies of the cross and whose destiny was destruction or ruin.

In similar fashion the writer of the Epistle to the Hebrews spoke of those who, rather than face the responsibility of relating themselves to Christ, shrink back to destruction. The word used in these passages and translated "destruction" or "perdition" does not involve the idea of annihilation. The idea is, rather, that the person goes on existing in a state that can be described only in terms of absolute ruin.

The eternal destiny of the wicked is also spoken of in terms of punishment. This punishment is a token of vengeance from God upon those who turn from his offer of mercy in Christ and choose to go on in disobedience and sin (Heb. 10:30–31). Men may choose God's mercy in Christ or they may choose God's judgment upon their disobedience. To reject in deliberate fashion the offer of God's mercy is to choose the only alternative—God's judgment, which is spoken of in terms of vengeance. This punishment is eternal in nature. In Mark 3:29 Jesus spoke of "an eternal sin," a sin which by its very nature had no terminus. In like manner the punishment of the wicked is spoken of as punishment which by its nature has no terminus.

In Hebrews 10:26–31 the writer contrasted the conduct of those who rebelled against the leadership of Moses and those who rebel against the leadership of the Son of God. Those who rebelled against the leadership of Moses perished. Those who rebel against the leadership of the Son of God are worthy of much greater punishment. Their sin is such that it tramples underfoot the body of the Son of God, it looks upon his sacrificed blood as having no more significance than the blood of an animal killed in the street, and it insults the gracious Holy Spirit of God. Only punishment can be the just sentence for such conduct.

In Matthew 26:24 and Mark 14:21 Jesus underscored the matter of punishment for the wicked; he said that it would have been better for them if they had never been born at all. Never to have lived is better than to have lived and rejected God's mercy and grace. Paul emphasized this element of punishment when, in Romans 2:8–9, he spoke of wrath and anguish upon those who are not obedient to the truth and who are given to a life of evil.

The eternal destiny of the wicked is further spoken of in terms of outer darkness. In Matthew 25:30 Jesus spoke of the unfaithful servant who was cast into outer darkness where there was weeping and gnashing of teeth. He had concluded two other stories (Matt. 22:13 and 24:51) with the same expression. Something of the same idea is presented in 2 Peter 2:17 and Jude 13. The destiny of the wicked is spoken of in those verses as "the dark blackness forever." The dark represents the unknown; the unknown has always brought to man a sense of dread and fear. To think of a region which is absolutely beyond the reach of light and which is inhabited by those who wail and grind their teeth in agony is to think in terms of ultimate dread.

The eternal destiny of the wicked is finally described in terms of fire. In Luke 16:19–31 the rich man indicated in his own words that he was tormented in flames. His condition is more graphically presented in his request that Lazarus be sent to dip but the tip of his finger in water and apply that to the parched tongue of the rich man to impart some relief from the torment. In Matthew 18:8–9 and Mark 9:43–48 the fire of eternal punishment is qualified by the term "unquenchable." The Greek adjective is the word which is transliterated into English as "asbestos." Asbestos is that which cannot be destroyed by fire. The Greek word meant fire which could not be extinguished.

This fire is spoken of in Jude 23 as devouring fire, and the same term is used in Hebrews 10:27, "the fierceness of fire which shall devour the adversary." "Devour" cannot mean "destroy" if this is an eternal condition. It is rather the fire which devours but never destroys. The last terrible picture of the fate of the wicked is presented in Revelation 20:14–15 and 21:8 as a lake of fire that burns with brimstone. There the wicked, in association with the devil and his evil agents, shall experience their eternal destiny.

What is the meaning of all of this? Even to read these New Testament passages is to experience a sense of dread and revolt against the entire concept. One who preaches on the subject of hell without a broken heart has not learned what the subject really means in Christian thought. So strong is man's revolt against the idea that even in the presence of these passages in the New Testament many have denied the reality of hell and have sought to explain in some other way the destiny of the wicked beyond this life.

It is quite common today to hear outright denial of any concept of punishment for the wicked. Other people believe that whatever punishment the future holds for the wicked will be punishment by which their condition will be remedied; ultimately they too will enjoy a state of blessedness. The doctrines of annihilationism and of universalism are very popular today. They are popular because something in the mind of man revolts at the picture of eternal punishment. After a survey of religious leaders (Catholic, non-Catholic, and Jewish) one writer [8] came to the conclusion that among the major religious groups related to the Jewish or Christian faith there are only three that hold to the idea of hell as a place of punishment— Roman Catholics, Lutherans, and Baptists. Strange company indeed! Even that conclusion must be qualified with the realization that there are many in these groups who have given up the idea of eternal punishment.

If one feels impelled by the New Testament to hold that

[8] George W. Cornell, "Hell-Fire Fades, Flares, in Church Opinions," *Star-Telegram* (Forth Worth), February 23, 1956.

hell is a place of eternal punishment, how is the fact of hell to be understood? It must be understood in the light of New Testament teachings on man's sin and rebellion against God, God's offer of mercy through the redemptive work of his Son in his incarnation, crucifixion, and resurrection, and man's rejection of God's grace and his choice of the way of Satan rather than the way of God. Man has made his own choice. God has done all that he could, consistent with his righteous character, to win man from rebellion and save him from that awful destiny. A person who would deny the literal nature of all of the punishment prepared for the wicked, finding difficulties in such apparently opposite terms as "the blackness of darkness" and "the devouring fire," can take little comfort in avoiding the literal if he understands that reality is always worse than representation. If hell is the kind of place that is represented in the New Testament, how unspeakably terrible is the reality of that fate.

Moreover, if this is true, how tremendous is the challenge to those entrusted with the responsibility of presenting to man the full truth of the significance of life, destiny, sin, and salvation. This has been historically and must ever be a part of the imperative of Christian missions and evangelism. To redeemed men God has entrusted the responsibility of presenting to the unredeemed the gospel of redemptive love, which can transform life here and now in this world. At the same time this gospel can prepare men for that which is beyond this life so that his eternal destiny will not be in that dread condition and company.

The Eternal Destiny of the Righteous

It is to life after death that man looks when he begins to consider the nature of life and destiny. His question is always, "What is that life like?" Man's dreams of what that life will be like have often gone far beyond that which is given by revelation from God. Christians look with disfavor on the sensual views of future survival in some religious systems, but at the same time many so-called Christian concepts come close to that same sensual idea. Islam looks upon man's future life as one in which he shall be married to large-eyed maidens and shall drink of a wine which results neither in headache nor dimmed wits. There are times when a Christian's description of his idea of heaven would be much like that. Knowledge of life after death must be derived from the New Testament. What then may be known about that life?

Abode of the righteous.—What is the place of the eternal home of the righteous? In contrast to that of the wicked, the righteous are spoken of as being with God, or in a relationship of blessedness and fellowship with God. Jesus appeared to have this in mind when he spoke of Lazarus as being "in Abraham's bosom" (Luke 16:19–31). Surely it was something of this that Jesus had in mind when he said in Matthew 25:21, "Enter into the joy of your Lord" and in Matthew 25:34, "Inherit the kingdom of my Father." Some of the blessedness of that idea is represented, too, in Jesus' statement in John 17:24, "You may be with me where I am."

Paul, in 1 Thessalonians 4:17, spoke of this being with the Lord as the destiny of the Lord's people beyond the second coming. He no longer saw two groups—the living and the dead—waiting for that glorious event but one raised and transformed group eternally in the Lord's presence. In 2 Corinthians 5:8 he voiced his assurance that to depart this life was to be at home with the Lord and expressed the same confidence in Philippians 1:23 when as a prisoner he spoke of death as a departure to be with Christ. All of this seems sufficient representation of the idea which is found throughout the New Testament that beyond this life the righteous shall live in a state of unhindered and uninterrupted fellowship with their Lord.

The place of the eternal abode of the righteous is spoken of as heaven. This word comes from the Greek noun οὐρανός, which was derived from a verb stem meaning "to encompass" or "to cover." It is the Greek equivalent for the Hebrew *shamayim*, which means "the upper regions" or "the heights above." Man, looking up to God, sees the place of God's dwelling and of man's eternal dwelling with him as being heaven, the heights above.

Jesus, in Luke 15:7, spoke of joy in heaven over one who repents. Apparently it was the joy of the eternal God that he had in mind. Heaven, then, is spoken of as the place of God's abode. This same idea is presented in John 14:1–2 by the reference to "my Father's house." In this passage there is the beautifully suggestive statement of Jesus, who for thirty years had been a carpenter, that he was going away to build dwelling places for the eternal habitation of his people. According to Hebrews 9:23–24, following his death and resurrection Jesus entered heaven to appear before the face of God in carrying on his work of priestly intercession. Here again heaven is the place of God's dwelling.

In this same epistle the place of man's eternal home is spoken of as a heavenly country and an abiding city. This was most meaningful to the Jewish readers with the background of their history, including slavery in Egypt, exile in Babylon, and now dispersion as a nation with the city of Jerusalem laid waste. The eyes of those who belonged to the Lord were turned to the future. With Abraham they looked for a city whose builder and maker is God—a strong contrast to the temporary tents of this life (Heb. 11:10). With other great people of their history they looked for a heavenly country in which God had prepared for them a city—a strong contrast to the wanderings over the earth which they had known (Heb. 11:13–16). The heavenly Jerusalem is Mount Zion, the very abode of God himself (Heb. 12:22). If, as many interpreters hold, the Epistle to the Hebrews was written after the destruction of Jerusalem in A.D. 70, these references to heaven as an abiding city for eternal dwelling are all the more forceful.

Heaven, as the ultimate home of the redeemed, is also found in the thinking of Peter. He spoke of the believer's incorruptible inheritance in heaven (1 Peter 1:3-4). He voiced his confidence in the coming of a new heaven (2 Peter 3:13) in relationship to the passing of the present order and the coming of the eternal order.

Paul too spoke of heaven as the ultimate home of the redeemed. The Christian's citizenship is in heaven (Phil. 3:20); hope is laid up for them in heaven (Col. 1:5); their Master is in heaven (Col. 4:1; Eph. 6:9); they have in the heavens an eternal house which shall be the dwelling place of the spirit (2 Cor. 5:1). References to the use of this concept could be multiplied. These appear to be sufficient indication that the New Testament writers, when they considered the ultimate home of the redeemed, thought in exalted terms of "the heights above," "the upper regions," that is, heaven.

Experience of the righteous.—What is the nature of the life and experience of the righteous? Again, in striking contrast to the destiny of the unrighteous there is an emphasis on the concept of "life" as the ultimate destiny of the righteous. This is life of a quality that transcends that which has been known here; it is life in the most complete sense. The New Testament speaks of the believer's entering this experience of life when by faith he relates himself to Christ. That does not mean that he comes to know here in this world all that is to be known. It means that he experiences, in reality, the transcendent life of Christ which will come to the complete state in the experience of the resurrection. This idea is plainly stated by Barth; [9] in his words one who believes Paul's statement (that if we

[9] Karl Barth, *Dogmatics in Outline* (New York: Philosophical Library, 1949), p. 155.

died with Christ we shall also live with him) has already
started here and now to live the complete life. That beginning
is not interrupted by death. That life is a continuing life
which begins now and finds its completion in the resurrection.
It can be known as "eternal life."

Space prohibits listing here the references in which the adjective "eternal" is used to qualify this life. The term was used
by Jesus in the Synoptic Gospels [10] and in John's Gospel.[11] It
was also used in Acts,[12] Hebrews,[13] and 1 Peter,[14] and it also
occupies an important place in the writings of Paul.[15] Even
though in the New Testament there is a strong emphasis on
quality in the use of the word, the concept of duration cannot
be removed from it. It retains in the New Testament that force
which it had in classical and popular usage. The ultimate destiny of the righteous is a higher level of life which never ends.

The transcendent nature of the lasting experience of the
righteous is reflected in other ways in the New Testament.
Jesus, in controversy with the Sadducees, indicated that life
after the resurrection will not be a restoration to the type
of life and experience which has been known here. It will be
a life which, in its relationships and nature, will transcend this
life and can more properly be described by the type of life
and experience known by the spirit servants of God, the angels (Matt. 22:30; Mark 12:25; Luke 20:36). Jesus' statement
in Matthew 25:34, "Come, you blessed," emphasizes this concept of transcendence. "Blessed" is the word that speaks of
the highest good. It speaks of the most desirable state to which
one may come and describes a state which man looks upon as

[10] Luke 10:25 ff.; 16:9; 18:18, 29; Mark 10:17, 30; Matt. 19:16, 29.
[11] John 3:15–16; 4:14, 36; 5:24, 39; 6:27, 40, 47, 50–51, 54, 57–58, 68;
8:51; 10:28; 11:25–26; 12:50; 17:3.
[12] Acts 13:46, 48.
[13] Hebrews 5:9; 9:12, 15; 10:34–35.
[14] 1 Peter 1:3–4; 5:4.
[15] Rom. 2:7; 6:23; 8:10; Gal. 6:7–9; 1 Cor. 15:42–57; 2 Cor. 5:1; 1 Tim.
1:16; 6:12; 2 Tim. 1:10; Titus 1:2; 3:7.

calling forth highest congratulations. Whatever that ultimate experience of the righteous shall be, it will be one which is lacking at no point in blessedness for the individual who has believed in Jesus.

The ultimate home of the righteous is spoken of as rest. This idea is most graphically presented in Hebrews 3:11, 18; 4:1, 3, 8–9. After wandering in the wilderness for forty years following their slavery in Egypt, ancient Israel looked eagerly to a permanent home in a land where they could cease their wanderings and live in peace and enjoyment. Their experience is an illustration of God's ultimate purpose for his people. God finished his work of creation and rested. Christ finished his work of re-creation—that is, redemption—and rested. When Christ's people have finished their work, there is a "sabbath kind of rest" waiting for them. The land of rest to which they look is illustrated by the land of rest to which ancient Israel looked.

This idea of rest is also found in Revelation 14:13. Here is the strangest beatitude of all those in the New Testament: "Blessed are the dead who die in the Lord . . . that they may rest from their labor, for their works follow them." All the beatitudes of Jesus are paradoxical in nature. They present ideas that are strange to the minds of men—blessed are the poor, blessed are those who hunger, blessed are those who mourn. From man's viewpoint the strangest of all is this statement, "Blessed are the dead." It must be noted, however, that it is a particular class of the dead who are thus pronounced blessed, and there is a special reason for it. Those who die in the Lord are blessed, and the reason for that blessedness is that they obtain the refreshment of rest after the toil of this life. At the same time their work does not stop when they stop; only the final day of God's judgment can determine what the full extent of the good of that work has been. To obtain rest in the eternal state does not mean to come to idleness. It does mean to come to renewed strength and refreshment after the toil of this life.

The most beautiful description of the ultimate home of the redeemed is reserved for the end of the New Testament, Revelation 21:1 to 22:5. Exiled on Patmos during the persecution of the Christians under the Emperor Domitian, John saw a vision of the living Christ, who gave to him a message of comfort and assurance for the beaten and broken Christians of that day. It assured them that the cause of Christ would be triumphant over Rome and that the forces of evil under the leadership of Satan would ultimately be defeated. It spoke of the ultimate home of the people of Christ in fellowship with him beyond this earthly stage of activity. The description of that ultimate home is given in three beautiful and meaningful pictures.[16]

John saw heaven as a tabernacle (21:1–8). In reality it was a new heaven and a new earth which John saw replacing the first heaven and the first earth. The statement in verse 1, "I saw a new heaven and a new earth," and the statement in verse 2, "I saw the holy city, New Jerusalem, coming down out of heaven," have been made the basis for lengthy conjecture as to the consummation of God's purpose for creation. Linking this passage with Romans 8:19–25 and 2 Peter 3:7–13, some interpreters have come to the conclusion that heaven, man's ultimate home, will be here in a restored and cleansed universe. They find the Romans 8 passage indicating that ultimately the material universe itself is to be set free from the condition into which it was plunged by the fall (Gen. 3:17); it will be set free through the cleansing and purging process of fire in the 2 Peter passage. This purged and restored earth will be the "new heaven and new earth" of Revelation 21.

This view is not limited to one particular approach to es-

[16] Cf. Ray Summers, *Worthy Is the Lamb* (Nashville: Broadman Press, 1951), pp. 211–15.

chatology. Men who are as far apart in their eschatological views as Larkin [17] and Carroll [18] both hold to this idea. New Testament references of this nature are sufficient for interesting speculation about the future but insufficient for such building of definite ideas or conclusions.

In Revelation 21:1 the word translated "new" is the Greek καινός. Two words, in the main, in Greek are translated "new" in English. One has the force of that which is new in time; the other has the force of that which is new in kind. It is this second word which is used throughout this passage when reference is made to a new heaven and a new earth. It is a new kind of heaven and earth which is the dwelling place for God's people.

The expression in verse 1, "the sea is no more," suggests that in this new kind of heaven and earth separation will be known no more. Earlier, in Revelation 4:6, the sea was a symbol of separation, of that which stood between the worshiper and God. In this new heaven and earth there will be nothing to stand between a man and his God.

John heard a voice from the throne itself saying, "Look, God's tabernacle is with men and he will dwell with them." In the Old Testament the tabernacle was God's meeting place with his people. In Revelation the idea seems to be that God will pitch his tent and dwell immediately and in intimate fellowship with his people. He will remove from them every indication of the distressing experiences which are known in this life, that is, weeping, pain, and death (vv. 3–4). These are not to be known in that new heaven and earth; all these things have ended with the old order.

A striking statement is found in verse 5. The One who occupies the throne, the reigning God of Revelation 4, no doubt,

[17] Clarence Larkin, *The Book of Revelation* (Philadelphia: Moyer and Lotter, 1919), pp. 195–210.

[18] B. H. Carroll, "The Book of Revelation," *An Interpretation of the English Bible* (New York: Fleming H. Revell Co., 1913).

says again, "Look, I am making everything new." He is making a new heaven and earth, one that will be different from this one, one that cannot be touched by the defiling presence of sin or the distressing presence of grief, one in which there will be nothing to separate him from his people. He shall dwell with them in immediate and perfect fellowship. This will be heaven indeed.

John saw heaven as a city (21:9–27). The second picture which is given of the ultimate home of the redeemed is that of a beautiful city. John was carried by the Spirit to the top of a high mountain where he saw the holy city, Jerusalem, coming down as beautiful as a bride adorned for her husband. The glory of God, like the jasper stone of chapter 4, was upon this city (v. 11). The city was a perfect cube twelve thousand furlongs wide, twelve thousand furlongs long, and twelve thousand furlongs high.

The walled city in that day was for the purpose of protecting the people. Such walls as those here described would speak in terms of perfect protection. The spaciousness of the city is seen in its measurement: the perfect symbolic number, one thousand, was multiplied by the perfect religious number, twelve, to present a perfect cube measuring twelve thousand furlongs each way. This is not to be regarded as a literal measurement of the city so that the possible occupancy could be determined by reducing the figures to cubic feet, though some have attempted that! The perfect number of such high dimensions is for the purpose of indicating the absolute in spaciousness. There will be room for all of God's people.

This city had twelve gates. There were three gates on either side of the city. Each gate was one huge pearl. The gates were not closed by day, and there was no night there; hence they stood open continuously. Many interesting suggestions are found in these symbols. First, there is abundant entrance into this city by a perfect number of gates, twelve, a perfect number for each side of the city, three, and the gates are never closed. A gate or a door is in size proportionate to the space that it serves. Imagine a wall fifteen hundred miles long and fifteen hundred miles high. Imagine three gates to serve such a wall. The impression is that of tremendous gates, and each gate was one huge pearl (v. 21). Pearls are produced out of the suffering of the oyster. Thus, in beautiful symbol, is presented the truth that the way into the eternal city is the suffering of the one who was himself the Pearl of great price.

One of the most forceful suggestions in all the symbolism of this city is that of beauty. The twelve foundations of the city were twelve precious stones. The walls gleamed crystal clear like a jasper stone. The streets were of gold so highly refined that it was as clear as transparent glass. Such beauty and purity stagger the imagination of man. There is no need of sacrifice in the city, so the Lord God the Almighty and the Lamb come to be the only sanctuary of God's people. They, too, are the illuminating power of this city, which needs neither sun nor moon. All the splendid pageantry of an oriental city on display with kings and their courts is used to describe the glory of this city (v. 24). Heaven, as John saw it, is a perfect city, offering for God's people an abundant entrance, perfect beauty, and perfect protection.

John saw heaven as a garden (22:1–5). The closing picture of man's ultimate home is presented in terms of a garden. The word "garden" (paradise) is not used in this passage, but everything descriptive of a garden was there, including the tree of life which, according to Revelation 2:7, grows in the garden of God. In this garden the stream which was the water of life has its source in the throne of God and the Lamb. Growing in this garden was the tree of life, bearing a different kind of fruit each month of the year and having leaves with healing properties for the health of the inhabitants of the garden.

Here in forceful symbol is answered man's question, "How can one live forever?" The necessities of the sustained life are here presented in the water of life, the fruit of the tree, and health through the healing property of the leaves. This does not mean that in that life man must drink of a magic stream of water or eat magic fruit or partake of magic leaves in order to live forever. Rather, this is a forceful way of saying that God has the ability to provide all that is needed to live forever.

The closing verses of the description of the garden are most instructive. Here is the throne of God and the Lamb, the central figures of this book, beginning with chapter 4. There is no curse in this garden. The Lord's servants look upon his face and render their service to him, being identified as his. The garden is brilliantly flooded with light from the very source of light itself, the eternal God, who once spoke, "Let there be light." The contrast between this ultimate garden home of man and his first garden home in Eden is without parallel anywhere. Into that first garden home came the presence of sin to defile, to destroy fellowship, and to rob man of his home. When the curtain is drawn on that scene in Genesis 3, it is drawn on a very dark and gloomy picture. The garden is there, but man has been driven out. God is there, but man has been driven from his presence. The tree of life is there, but man is kept away from it by divine messengers with flaming swords. There is a curse upon man, upon woman, and upon the garden itself because of what sin has done.

In dramatic contrast observe the difference in this final garden home. God is in the garden, and man is in the immediate presence of God, looking upon his face and serving him. Rather than being driven away because of sin, man bears on his forehead the name which identifies him as belonging to God. There is no curse in this garden; that has been lifted through the redemptive work of the reigning God and the redeeming Lamb. Everything in this garden is bright and beautiful, flooded by the light of the eternal God himself. All that was lost to man in his first home, lost because of sin, because of disobedience, is restored to him in this final home, restored through righteousness and obedience—not his own righteousness and obedience but the righteousness and obedience of the Lamb who is the Christ.

What took place in a garden which is in the middle of the Bible made this change possible. That garden (John 18:1), which we know as Gethsemane, represents what has made possible the defeat of sin and the ultimate union of Christ with his people for eternity. In that garden Christ experienced an agony of suffering which was a part of the suffering that was to be his on the cross the next day. As he faced the shameful agony of that experience, he prayed that if there were any other way that redemption for man could be worked out, this way of the drinking of the cup of the cross might pass from him. At all times, however, he kept himself in the very center of the divine will in the prayer, "Not my will but thy will be done" (Matt. 26:39). Without his sacrifice there could be no eternal garden home for man.

Appendix I

Graph of Premillennial Adventism

I. Church Age (Rev. 1–3)	II. Great Tribulation (seven years) (Rev. 4:1–19:21)	III. Millennium (a thousand years) (Rev. 20:1–6)	IV. Little Time (Rev. 20:7–15)	V. Eternity (Rev. 21–22)
1. Increase of evil	1. "Rapture" coming of Christ *for* saints	1. "Revelation" coming of Christ *with* saints	1. Satan loosed	1. Wicked in hell
2. Failure of church	2. "Harvest" resurrection of saints	2. "Gleanings" resurrection of dead tribulation saints	2. Satan leads revolt	2. Righteous in heaven
	3. Church taken from world	3. Battle of Armageddon	3. Battle of Gog and Magog	
	4. Judgment seat of Christ (on believers)	4. Chaining of Satan	4. Satan defeated	
	5. Tribulation on Jews	5. Sheep and goat judgment on nations	5. Wicked raised	
		6. The millennial kingdom	6. Great white throne judgment on wicked	

I. The Church Age

This age extends from the time of Christ's establishing the church at his first coming until his "Rapture" coming to take the church away. It is characterized by two things:

1. The rapid increase of evil as the end nears
2. The failure of the church

II. The Great Tribulation

Some interpreters hold that this may come at any time; others think it cannot come until other prophecies have been fulfilled, such as the restoration of the Jewish nation in Palestine, the revival of the Roman (or Babylonian) Empire with its ruler as the antichrist, the supreme antidivine world power. This period will last seven years and is thus analyzed:

1. The "Rapture" coming of Christ not to the earth but in the air
2. The "Harvest" resurrection of the Old Testament saints and the church-age saints
3. The taking of the church and the Holy Spirit out of the earth to leave it in the grip of evil
4. The judgment-seat "sifting" of believers in heaven
5. The judgment of God upon the Jews by means of the great tribulation. The seven years are divided into two parts:
   (1) During the first three and one-half years the Jews, having returned to Palestine, will rebuild their Temple and reestablish the sacrifices of ancient Israel. The Roman ruler (antichrist) will permit this.
   (2) At the beginning of the second three and one-half years the Roman ruler will break his agreement with the Jews and demand that they worship him. Their refusal will bring on indescribable persecution. This will be the great tribulation pictured in Revelation. It will be God's judgment upon them for rejecting Christ. During this time the Jewish leaders will encourage their people by preaching the "gospel of the kingdom." This will not be the gospel of grace preached during the church age. It will be a message which proclaims that the Messiah is coming to deliver them. The Messiah for whom they look is *not* Jesus.

III. The Millennium

This is a period of a thousand years of the reign of peace and righteousness on earth. In brief, this is the analysis of events:

1. At the end of the seven years of great tribulation Christ will return *with* his saints in the "Revelation" part of the second coming.
2. He will raise from the dead those who during the tribulation became Christians and died; this is the "Gleanings" resurrection.
3. He will defeat antichrist at the Battle of Armageddon, bind Satan, and cast him into the abyss for a thousand years.
4. He will hold the sheep and goat judgment to determine which nations will be permitted to continue in the world during the millennium.
5. He will establish his millennial kingdom on earth with headquarters in Palestine. There he will rule the world through the twelve apostles and the Jews in Palestine and through the Christians throughout the world. The Jews will be the world-dominating nation and all other nations blessed through them. Since Satan is bound, good will dominate the world as men have one last chance to do right without Satan's influence. Four classes of people will live in the world.

    (1) Believers who were raised to their eternal bodies at the "Rapture" and "Revelation"

    (2) Believers who were living and transformed to their eternal bodies at the "Rapture"

    (3) Believers who became believers during the tribulation and are still in their mortal bodies, as well as the Jews who admitted their error and accepted Christ when he came at Armageddon

    (4) Unbelievers who pay "lip service" obedience to the rule of Christ but in their hearts are opposed to him

IV. The Little Time

This is described, as to duration, only by use of the New Testament term "a little time." It is a "little time" in contrast with the thousand years which precede it.

1. At the end of the thousand years Satan will be loosed to lead the "lip service" unbelievers in a revolt against the rule of Christ.
2. These unbelievers will prove to be as numerous as the sands of the sea. In their revolt they will lay siege to the capital city, Jerusalem, in the Battle of Gog and Magog.
3. They will be defeated and Satan will be cast into hell forever.
4. All the wicked of all the ages will be raised from the dead—"the second resurrection"—as well as believers who died during the millennium.
5. The great white throne judgment will be held upon the wicked only. It will take place in the air while the earth is being purged and renovated by fire.

V. Eternity

The great white throne judgment closes the present world order.
1. The wicked will be cast into hell forever.
2. The righteous will have their eternal home in heaven, which is here in a purged and renovated earth.

In the above system there are:
1. Two comings of Christ—the "Rapture" coming before the great tribulation; the "Revelation" coming seven years later.
2. Two resurrections (Christ's was the "first fruit"):
   (1) The first resurrection in two parts:
      a. Old Testament saints and church age saints at the "Rapture." This is called the "Harvest" resurrection.
      b. Tribulation saints at the end of the great tribulation. This is regarded as part of the first resurrection and is called the "Gleanings."
   (2) The second resurrection in two parts:
      a. Saints who died during the millennium are raised at the end of the millennium.
      b. The wicked dead of all the ages are raised at the end of the millennium.
3. Five judgments:
   (1) Believers' sins judged at Calvary
   (2) Believers' works judged before judgment seat of Christ in heaven during the great tribulation
   (3) Jews judged by persecution during the great tribulation

(4) Nations judged on earth (sheep and goat judgment) before the millennium

(5) Wicked men judged in the air at the great white throne judgment after the millennium

The above analysis relates to the very fully worked out system sometimes called *dispensational premillennialism*. It is seen clearest in the previously cited works of Scofield, Larkin, Talbot, Chafer, and others.

Many interpreters are not in full accord with the details of the system and prefer a modified form of dispensational approach, sometimes called *historic premillennialism*. This is seen clearest in the previously cited works of Alford, Ladd, and others. This system holds to two resurrections: believers before the millennium; unbelievers after the millennium. It holds to separate judgments: believers before the judgment seat of Christ before the millennium; unbelievers at the great white throne after the millennium.

While there are many differences on fine points of interpretation, the system differs from dispensational premillennialism at two major points. First, it does not divide the second coming of Christ into two parts seven years removed. It holds that the "Rapture" is only the catching up of believers to welcome Christ in his "Revelation." All this is placed after the great tribulation. Second, this so-called *historic premillennialism* does not make a major place for the Jews as a nation during the millennium. For these interpreters, whatever the millennium is to be it will be *Christian*.

Appendix II
Graph of Postmillennial Adventism

I. Present World Order Gradually Becoming Millennium	II. Eternal Order
1. Good and evil continue together.	1. At end of the millennial reign of righteousness Christ returns.
2. Ultimately through the transforming power of the gospel evil is defeated and good reigns in the world —the millennium.	2. He raises all the dead.
	3. He holds final judgment.
	4. Wicked are consigned to hell.
	5. Righteous have their eternal home in heaven.

I. The Millennium

As noted above, the transforming power of the gospel is destined ultimately to result in the defeat of evil and the rule of righteousness in the world. From his throne in heaven Christ carries on this battle. His soldiers (Christians) in the world "fight" as they declare the gospel truth. By this means the apostate Roman Catholic Church will be destroyed. The Jews, having returned to Palestine, will be attacked by enemy nations. God will intervene and rescue them. They will turn and accept the lordship of Christ—a nation in a day. This nation of "Pauls" preaching the gospel of grace will usher in the millennium. There will be

1. A thousand years of the possession of the earth by the saints— no war, no pestilence, no false religion. The righteous will be in charge of world government.

2. Evil will be in the world but will be almost nonexistent compared to good.

3. Men will subdue the earth, as God commanded, to such extent that all the earth will be as habitable as a paradise.

4. Near the end of this period Christians will become careless and lax, taking their position for granted. Satan will reassert himself and try to enlist the loyalty and worship of men.

II. The Eternal Age

At the end of this millennial age as Satan reasserts himself

1. Christ will return in his second coming.

2. He will defeat Satan and cast him into hell.

3. He will raise all the dead at one time—righteous and wicked.

4. He will judge all men at one time.

5. He will consign the wicked to hell.

6. He will give to the righteous their eternal home—heaven.

Appendix III
Graph of Nonmillennial Adventism

I. Present World Order	II. Eternal Order
	1. Second coming of Christ
	2. Resurrection of all
	3. Judgment upon all
	4. Eternal Order:
	(1) Hell for wicked
	(2) Heaven for righteous

I. The Present World Order

This present world order will continue with good and evil existing until the end, i.e., until the second coming of Christ. It is material and temporal in nature and cannot endure forever.

II. The Eternal Order

1. The second coming of Christ (which may be at any time) will become reality.
2. When he comes he will raise all the dead—one resurrection—righteous and wicked.
3. He will at that time execute judgment upon all—righteous and wicked—in one judgment.
4. He will consign the wicked to hell for eternity.
5. He will receive the righteous unto himself for their eternal home in heaven.

This system holds to one second coming of Christ, one resurrection, one judgment, thus ending the world order and establishing the eternal order without the interim of a millennial order. For the meaning of the millennium according to this view see pages 89–90 of this book. See also *Worthy Is the Lamb*, pages 204–206.

Bibliography

BOOKS

ALFORD, HENRY. "The Acts of the Apostles, the Epistles to the Romans and Corinthians." (Vol. II, *The Expositor's Greek Testament*, edited by W. Robertson Nicoll.) Cambridge: Deighton, Bell, and Co., 1871.

ALLIS, OSWALD T. *Prophecy and the Church*. Philadelphia: Presbyterian and Reformed Publishing Company, 1945.

BAILEY, JOHN W. "The Epistles to the Philippians, Colossians, First and Second Thessalonians, First and Second Timothy, Titus, Philemon, Hebrews." (Vol. XI, *The Interpreter's Bible*, edited by George Arthur Buttrick.) New York: Abingdon Press, 1955.

BAILLIE, JOHN. *And the Life Everlasting*. New York: Charles Scribner's Sons, 1933.

————. *The Belief in Progress*. New York: Charles Scribner's Sons, 1951.

BARNES, ALBERT. *Notes on the New Testament: Matthew-Mark*. Grand Rapids: Baker Book House, 1949.

————. *Notes on the New Testament: The First Epistle to the Corinthians*. Grand Rapids: Baker Book House, 1949.

BARTH, KARL. *Dogmatics in Outline*. Translated by G. T. Thomason. New York: Philosophical Library, 1949.

————. *The Resurrection of the Dead*. New York: Fleming H. Revell Co., 1933.

BEASLEY-MURRAY, G. R. *Jesus and the Future*. London: Macmillan and Co., Ltd., 1954.

BERNARD, J. H. "The Second Epistle to the Corinthians, Epistles to the Galatians, Ephesians, Philippians, Colossians." (Vol. III, *The Expositor's Greek Testament*, edited by W. Robertson Nicoll.) Grand Rapids: Wm. B. Eerdmans Publishing Co., n.d.

BLISS, GEORGE R. "Commentary on the Gospel of Luke." (Vol. II, *An American Commentary on the New Testament*, edited by Alvah Hovey.) Philadelphia: American Baptist Publication Society, 1881.

BROADUS, JOHN A. "Commentary on the Gospel of Matthew." (Vol. I, *An American Commentary on the New Testament*, edited by Alvah Hovey.) Philadelphia: American Baptist Publication Society, 1886.

BRUNNER, EMIL. *Eternal Hope*. Philadelphia: The Westminster Press, 1954.

————. *The Great Invitation*. London: Lutterworth Press, 1955.

————. *Man in Revolt*. Philadelphia: The Westminster Press, 1947.

————. *Our Faith*. New York: Charles Scribner's Sons, 1936.

CALVIN, JOHN. *Commentaries on the Epistle of Paul the Apostle to the Romans*, edited by John Owen. Grand Rapids: Wm. B. Eerdmans Publishing Co., 1947.

————. *Commentary on the Epistles of Paul to the Corinthians*, edited by John Pringle. Grand Rapids: Wm. B. Eerdmans Publishing Co., 1948.

————. *Commentary on the Epistles of Paul the Apostle to the Philippians, Colossians, and Thessalonians*, edited by John Pringle. Grand Rapids: Wm. B. Eerdmans Publishing Co., 1948.

CARROLL, B. H. "The Book of Revelation," *An Interpretation of the English Bible*, edited by J. B. Cranfill. New York: Fleming H. Revell Co., 1913.

————. "The Four Gospels," *An Interpretation of the English Bible*, edited by J. B. Cranfill. New York: Fleming H. Revell Co., 1916.

————. "James, I and II Thessalonians and I and II Corinthians," *An Interpretation of the English Bible*, edited by J. B. Cranfill. New York: Fleming H. Revell, Co., 1916.

CHAFER, LEWIS SPERRY. *Major Bible Themes*. Chicago: Moody Press, 1926.

————. *Systematic Theology*. Dallas: Dallas Seminary Press, 1948.

CHARLES, R. H. *A Critical History of the Doctrine of a Future Life in Israel, in Judaism, and in Christianity*. (2d ed.) London: Adam and Charles Black, 1913.

————. *Religious Development Between the Old and New Testaments*. New York: Henry Holt & Co., Inc., n.d.

————. "The Revelation of St. John," *The International Critical Commentary*. New York: Charles Scribner's Sons, 1950.

The Classical Latin Dictionary. New York: Hinds, Hayden and Eldredge, Inc., n.d.

CONNER, W. T. *The Resurrection of Jesus.* Nashville: Sunday School
Board of the Southern Baptist Convention, 1926.

CONZELMANN, HANS. *Die Mitte der Zeit.* Tübingen: J. C. B. Mohr
(Paul Siebeck), 1954.

CRAIG, CLARENCE TUCKER. "The First Epistle to the Corinthians."
(Vol. X, *The Interpreter's Bible,* edited by George Arthur Buttrick.) New York: Abingdon-Cokesbury Press, 1953.

CULLMANN, OSCAR. *Christ and Time.* London: Student Christian
Movement Press, Ltd., 1952.

————. *The State in the New Testament.* New York: Charles Scribner's Sons, 1956.

DAVIES, W. D., ANḃ DAUBE, D. (eds.). *The Background of the New
Testament and Its Eschatology.* Cambridge: Cambridge University Press, 1956.

DENNY, JAMES. "The Second Epistle to the Corinthians." (Vol. V,
The Expositor's Bible, edited by W. Robertson Nicoll.) New York:
Eaton and Mains, n.d.

DODS, MARCUS. "The Gospel of St. John." (Vol. I, *The Expositor's
Greek Testament,* edited by W. Robertson Nicoll.) Grand Rapids:
Wm. B. Eerdmans Publishing Co., n.d.

ECKMAN, GEORGE P. *When Christ Comes Again.* New York: Abingdon Press, 1918.

ELLICOTT, CHARLES JOHN. *Commentary on the Whole Bible,* Vol. VI.
Grand Rapids: Zondervan Publishing House, 1954.

ERDMAN, CHARLES R. *The Second Epistle of Paul to the Corinthians.*
Philadelphia: The Westminster Press, 1929.

FINDLAY, G. G. "The Acts of the Apostles, St. Paul's Epistle to the
Romans, St. Paul's First Epistle to the Corinthians." (Vol. II,
The Expositor's Greek Testament, edited by W. Robertson Nicoll.)
Grand Rapids: Wm. B. Eerdmans Publishing Co., n.d.

GLOEGE, GERHARD. *Das Reich Gottes im Neuen Testament.* Leipzig:
Borna, 1928.

GOODSPEED, CALVIN. *Messiah's Second Advent: A Study in Eschatology.* Toronto: William Briggs, 1900.

GOUDGE, HENRY LEIGHTON. "The First Epistle to the Corinthians,"
Westminster Commentaries, edited by Walter Lack. London:
Methuen and Co., Ltd., 1928.

GOULD, E. P. "Epistles to the Corinthians, Galatians, Ephesians, Philippians, Colossians, Thessalonians." (Vol. V, *An American Commentary on the New Testament,* edited by Alvah Hovey.) Philadelphia: American Baptist Publication Society, 1887.

HACKETT, HORATIO B. "A Commentary on the Acts of the Apostles." (Vol. IV, *An American Commentary on the New Testament,* edited by Alvah Hovey.) Philadelphia: American Baptist Publication Society, 1882.

HALL, FRANCIS J. "Eschatology," *Dogmatic Theology.* New York: Longmans, Green and Co., 1922.

HAMILTON, FLOYD E. *The Basis of Christian Faith.* New York: George H. Doran Company, 1927.

————. *The Basis of Millennial Faith.* Grand Rapids: Wm. B. Eerdmans Publishing Co., 1942.

HART, J. H. A. "The First and Second Epistles General of Peter, the Epistles of John, the General Epistle of Jude, Revelation of St. John the Divine." (Vol. V, *The Expositor's Greek Testament,* edited by W. Robertson Nicoll.) Grand Rapids: Wm. B. Eerdmans Publishing Co., n.d.

HAYES, DOREMUS A. *The Resurrection Fact.* Nashville: Cokesbury Press, 1932.

HENDRIKSEN, WILLIAM. "Exposition of I and II Thessalonians," *New Testament Commentary.* Grand Rapids: Baker Book House, 1955.

————. "Exposition of the Gospel According to John," *New Testament Commentary.* Grand Rapids: Baker Book House, 1953.

HODGE, ARCHIBALD ALEXANDER. *Outlines of Theology.* New York: Robert Carter and Brothers, 1882.

HODGE, CHARLES. *An Exposition of the First Epistle to the Corinthians.* Grand Rapids: Wm. B. Eerdmans Publishing Co., 1950.

HODGES, JESSE WILSON. *Christ's Kingdom and Coming.* Grand Rapids: Wm. B. Eerdmans Publishing Co., 1957.

HOVEY, ALVAH. *Biblical Eschatology.* Philadelphia: American Baptist Publication Society, 1888.

————. "Commentary on the Gospel of John." (Vol. III, *An American Commentary on the New Testament,* edited by Alvah Hovey.) Philadelphia: American Baptist Publication Society, 1885.

HOWARD, WILBERT F. "The Gospel According to St. John." (Vol. VIII, *The Interpreter's Bible,* edited by George Arthur Buttrick.) Nashville: Abingdon Press, 1952.

HUNTER, ARCHIBALD M. "The Epistles of James, First and Second Peter, First, Second and Third John, Jude, and the Revelation." (Vol. XII, *The Interpreter's Bible*, edited by George Arthur Buttrick.) New York: Abingdon Press, 1957.

JOHNSON, SHERMAN E. "The Gospel According to St. Matthew." (Vol. VI, *The Interpreter's Bible*, edited by George A. Buttrick.) New York: Abingdon Press, 1951.

JONES, RUSSELL BRADLEY. *The Things Which Shall Be Hereafter.* Nashville: Broadman Press, 1947.

KANTONEN, T. A. *The Christian Hope.* Philadelphia: Muhlenberg Press, 1954.

KEIM, KARL. *Jesus von Nazara.* Publisher's data not available.

KENNEDY, H. A. A. "The Second Epistle to the Corinthians, Epistles to the Galatians, Ephesians, Philippians, Colossians." (Vol. III, *The Expositor's Greek Testament,* edited by W. Robertson Nicoll.) Grand Rapids: Wm. B. Eerdmans Publishing Co., n.d.

KERR, HUGH THOMSON (ed.). *A Compend of Luther's Theology.* Philadelphia: The Westminster Press, 1943.

KIK, J. MARCELLUS. *Matthew Twenty-four.* Grand Rapids: Baker Book House, 1948.

———. *Revelation Twenty: An Exposition.* Philadelphia: Presbyterian and Reformed Publishing Company, 1955.

KLING, CHRISTIAN FRIEDRICK. "The First Epistle of Paul to the Corinthians," *A Commentary on the Holy Scriptures,* edited by John Peter Lange. New York: Charles Scribner's Sons, 1899.

KNUDSON, ALBERT C. *The Religious Teaching of the Old Testament.* New York: Abingdon-Cokesbury Press, 1918.

KROMMINGA, D. H. *The Millennium.* Grand Rapids: Wm. B. Eerdmans Publishing Co., 1948.

LADD, GEORGE E. *Crucial Questions About the Kingdom of God.* Grand Rapids: Wm. B. Eerdmans Publishing Co., 1954.

———. *The Blessed Hope.* Grand Rapids: Wm. B. Eerdmans Publishing Co., 1956.

LAKE, KIRSOPP. *The Historical Evidence for the Resurrection of Jesus Christ.* New York: G. P. Putnam's Sons, 1912.

LANGE, JOHN PETER. "The First Epistle of Paul to the Corinthians," *Critical Doctrinal and Homiletical Commentary.* New York: Charles Scribner's Sons, 1869.

LARKIN, CLARENCE. *The Book of Revelation.* Philadelphia: Rev. Clarence Larkin Estate, 1919.

LATHAM, HENRY. *The Risen Master*. Cambridge: Deighton Bell and Co., 1901.

LENSKI, R. C. H. *The Interpretation of St. Matthew's Gospel*. Columbus: Wartburg Press, 1943.

———. *The Interpretation of St. John's Gospel*. Columbus: Lutheran Book Concern, 1942.

———. *The Interpretation of St. John's Revelation*. Columbus: Wartburg Press, 1943.

———. *The Interpretation of St. Paul's Epistles to the Colossians, to the Thessalonians, to Timothy, to Titus and to Philemon*. Columbus: Wartburg Press, 1946.

———. *The Interpretation of St. Paul's Epistles to the Galatians, to the Ephesians and to the Philippians*. Columbus: Wartburg Press, 1946.

———. *The Interpretation of St. Paul's First and Second Epistles to the Corinthians*. Columbus: Wartburg Press, 1946.

LIDDELL, HENRY GEORGE, AND SCOTT, ROBERT. *A Greek-English Lexicon*. (7th ed.) New York: Harper and Brothers, 1883.

LIGHTFOOT, J. B. "Epistle to the Philippians," *The Epistles of St. Paul*. New York: The Macmillan Company, 1903.

LUTHER, MARTIN. *Luthers Werke*. Berlin: C. V. Schwetschke und Sohn, 1898.

McDOWELL, EDWARD A. *The Meaning and Message of the Book of Revelation*. Nashville: Broadman Press, 1951.

MACKINTOSH, H. R. *Immortality and the Future*. New York: Hodder and Stoughton, 1917.

———. "Thessalonians and Corinthians." *The Westminster New Testament*, edited by Alfred E. Garvie. New York: Fleming H. Revell Co., n.d.

MASSIE, J. "First and Second Corinthians," (Vol. VII, *The Century Bible*, edited by W. F. Adeney.) London: Caxton Publishing Co., n.d.

MILLIGAN, WILLIAM. *The Book of Revelation*. New York: A. C. Armstrong and Son, 1889.

MOULTON, JAMES HOPE, AND MILLIGAN, GEORGE. *The Vocabulary of the Greek New Testament Illustrated from the Papyri and Other Non-literary Sources*. Grand Rapids: Wm. B. Eerdmans Publishing Co., 1949.

MOULTON, W. F., AND GEDEN, A. S. *A Concordance to the Greek New Testament*. Edinburgh: T. and T. Clark, 1950.

MULLINS, EDGAR YOUNG. *Baptist Beliefs.* Philadelphia: Judson Press, 1951.

————. *The Christian Religion in Its Doctrinal Expression.* Philadelphia: Judson Press, 1938.

MURRAY, GEORGE L. *Millennial Studies, a Search for Truth.* Grand Rapids: Baker Book House, 1948.

NYGREN, ANDERS. *Commentary on Romans.* Philadelphia: Muhlenberg Press, 1949.

ORR, JAMES. *The Resurrection of Jesus.* London: Hodder and Stoughton, n.d.

OWEN, D. R. G. *Body and Soul.* Philadelphia: The Westminster Press, 1956.

PAULUS, HEINRICH EBERHARD GOTTLOB. *Das Leben Jesu.* Heidelberg: C. F. Winter, 1828.

PEROWNE, J. J. S. *The First Epistle to the Corinthians.* ("Cambridge Greek Testament for Schools and Colleges Series.") Cambridge: Cambridge University Press, 1886.

————. *The Second Epistle of Paul the Apostle to the Corinthians.* ("Cambridge Greek Testament for Schools and Colleges Series.") Cambridge: Cambridge University Press, 1892.

PIETERS, ALBERTUS. *The Lamb, the Woman and the Dragon.* Grand Rapids: Zondervan Publishing Company, 1937.

PLUMMER, A. *The Gospel According to St. John.* ("Cambridge Greek Testament for Schools and Colleges Series.") Cambridge: Cambridge University Press, 1896.

REICKE, BO. *The Disobedient Spirits and Christian Baptism.* Copenhagen: Ejnar Munksgaard, 1946.

ROBERTS, ALEXANDER, AND DONALDSON, JAMES. *The Ante-Nicene Fathers,* Vol. I. Grand Rapids: Wm. B. Eerdmans Publishing Co., 1956.

ROBERTSON, ARCHIBALD THOMAS. "The Epistles of Paul," *Word Pictures in the New Testament.* Nashville: Broadman Press, 1931.

SCHAFF, PHILIP. *The Creeds of Christendom.* New York: Harper and Brothers, 1919.

SCHLATTER, ADOLF. *Das Evangelist Johannes.* Stuttgart: Calwer Vereinsbuchhandlung, 1930.

SCOFIELD, C. I. *The Scofield Bible Correspondence Course,* Vol. II. Chicago: Moody Bible Institute, 1907.

————. *The Scofield Reference Bible.* New York: Oxford University Press, 1945.

A Short Exposition of Dr. Martin Luther's Small Catechism. St. Louis: Concordia Publishing House, 1912.

SKRINE, JOHN HUNTLEY. *The Gospel of the Manhood.* London: Skeffington and Son, Ltd., 1922.

SMITH, DAVID. "Acts of the Apostles; the Epistle of St. Paul to the Romans; to the First and Second Epistles of St. Paul to the Corinthians," *The Disciple's Commentary on the New Testament.* New York: Ray Long and Richard R. Smith, Inc., 1932.

———. *Commentary on the Four Gospels,* Vol. I. New York: Doubleday, Doran and Company, Inc., 1928.

SNOWDEN, JAMES H. *The Coming of the Lord: Will it Be Premillennial?* New York: The Macmillan Company, 1919.

STAFFORD, T. P. *A Study of the Kingdom.* Nashville: Sunday School Board of the Southern Baptist Convention, 1925.

STRACK, HERMANN L., AND BILLERBECK, PAUL. *Kommentar zum Neuen Testament aus Talmud und Midrash,* Vols. I and II. Munich: C. H. Becksche Verlagsbuchhandlung, 1924.

STRAUSS, DAVID FRIEDRICK. *A New Life of Jesus.* London: Williams and Norgate, 1879.

STRONG, AUGUSTUS HOPKINS. *Systematic Theology.* Philadelphia: Judson Press, 1942.

SUMMERS, RAY. *Worthy Is the Lamb.* Nashville: Broadman Press, 1951.

SWETE, HENRY BARCLAY. *The Apocalypse of St. John.* New York: The Macmillan Company, 1907.

———. *The Life of the World to Come.* New York: The Macmillan Company, 1917.

TALBOT, LOUIS T. *The Revelation of Jesus Christ.* Grand Rapids: Wm. B. Eerdmans Publishing Co., 1953.

THAYER, JOSEPH HENRY. *A Greek-English Lexicon of the New Testament.* New York: American Book Company, 1889.

TRENCH, G. H. *The Crucifixion and Resurrection of Jesus.* London: John Murray, 1908.

VOS, GEERHARDUS. *The Pauline Eschatology.* Grand Rapids: Wm. B. Eerdmans Publishing Co., 1953.

WEATHERHEAD, LESLIE D. *After Death.* Nashville: Abingdon-Cokesbury Press, 1936.

WEIZSÄCKER, CARL VON. *The Apostolic Age of the Christian Church.* Translated by James Millar. New York: G. P. Putnam's Sons, 1907.

WILLIAMS, CHARLES B. *A Commentary on the Pauline Epistles.* Chicago: Moody Press, 1953.

WILLIAMS, N. M. "Commentary on the Epistles of Peter." (Vol. VI, *An American Commentary on the New Testament,* edited by Alvah Hovey.) Philadelphia: American Baptist Publication Society, 1890.

ARTICLES IN JOURNALS AND ENCYCLOPEDIAS

BECKWITH, C. A. "Biblical Conceptions of Soul and Spirit," *The New Schaff-Herzog Encyclopedia of Religious Knowledge,* XI, 12–14. New York: Funk and Wagnalls Company, 1908.

BROYDE, ISSAC. "Soul," *The Jewish Encyclopedia,* XI, 472–76. New York: Funk and Wagnalls Company, 1901.

CARROLL, B. H. "The Second Advent and the Millennium," *The Baptist Standard* (Dallas), (February 18, 1904).

CORNELL, GEORGE W. "Hell-Fire Fades, Flares, in Church Opinions," *The Star-Telegram* (Fort Worth), February 23, 1956.

CORNFORD, F. M. "The Division of the Soul," *Hibbert Journal,* XXVIII (January, 1930), 206–19.

JEREMIAS, JOACHIM. "Flesh and Blood Cannot Inherit the Kingdom of God," *New Testament Studies,* II (February, 1956), 151–59.

KELLOGG, S. H. "Trichotomy: A Biblical Study," *Bibliotheca Sacra.* XLVII, 1890.

LAIDLAW, J. "Body" (I, 309), "Soul" (IV, 608), "Spirit" (IV, 611–12), *A Dictionary of the Bible,* edited by James Hastings. New York: Charles Scribner's Sons, 1905.

ROBINSON, H. W. "Hebrew Psychology in Relation to Pauline Anthropology," *Mansfield College Essays.* 1909.

SEVENSTER, J. N. "Einige Bemerkungen 'über den "Zwischenzustand" bei Paulus,'" *New Testament Studies,* I (May, 1955), 291–96.

WALSH, CHAD. "Last Things, First Things," *Theology Today,* VI (April, 1949), 25–26.

Scripture Index

228

Index